SAMMY!

Partap Sharma is a playwright, novelist (*Days of the Turban*) and author of four books for children. His best-known plays include: *A Touch of Brightness* (initially banned but reprieved seven years later by the judgement of the Bombay High Court); *Power Play*; *Begum Sumroo*; and *Zen Katha*. His plays have been staged in various countries and his books have been published in India, Britain, USA, France, Denmark, Holland and Canada.

As an actor, he has played the lead in five Hindi feature films and won the National Award in 1971 for his performance in the award-winning *Phir Bhi*. He has also played the role of Nehru in the film *Nehru: Jewel of India*. In the year 2002, he spent three months in China to take part, again as Nehru, in an international film originally titled *The Bandung Sonata* and subsequently re-titled for release in China as *Chou-en-lai in Bandung*.

He has directed a number of documentary films: *The Framework of Famine* (banned for a while and then released on proviso that it never goes abroad); *The Burning Question* (banned altogether); and *Kamli*. He co-directed *Viewpoint Amritsar*. He has also produced and directed a historical series, which was telecast at primetime over Channel Four Television, London, titled *The Raj Through Indian Eyes*. The Museum of the British Empire & Commonwealth, in Bristol, now has a permanent section devoted to film clips and interviews titled *The Partap Sharma Archive on the British Raj*. His voice is well-known to cinema, TV and radio audiences as he is one of India's foremost commentators and narrators.

SAMMY!

A play in two acts

Partap Sharma

Rupa & Co

in association with
GANDHI SMARAK NIDHI, MUMBAI

*This play is dedicated to the
memory of Vithalbhai K. Jhaveri,
Dr. Usha Mehta
and all their colleagues, past and present,
at the Mani Bhavan Gandhi Sangrahalaya,
Laburnum Road, Mumbai,
and to Peter Rühe of
GandhiServe e.K. (Berlin).*

Copyright © Partap Sharma 2005

First Published 2005
Third Impression 2011

Published by
Rupa Publications India Pvt. Ltd.
7/16, Ansari Road, Daryaganj
New Delhi 110 002

Sales Centres:
Allahabad Bengaluru Chandigarh Chennai
Hyderabad Jaipur Kathmandu
Kolkata Mumbai

All rights reserved.
No part of this publication may be reproduced, stored in a retrieval
system, or transmitted, in any form or by any means, electronic,
mechanical, photocopying, recording or otherwise,
without the prior permission of the publishers.

Typeset in 11 pts. Palm Springs by
Mindways Design

Printed in India by
Saurabh Printers Pvt. Ltd.

CONTENTS

Acknowledgements	*viii*
Cast	3
Act One	5
Act Two	73

ACKNOWLEDGEMENTS

In arriving at the final draft of the play, I was helped by the comments and keen response of the audience at Brockwood Park School, U.K., where, as a visitor, I was invited to read out the first draft of the script in 2001.

Subsequently, I was encouraged by the discerning participation in a dramatized public reading at the Yatra restaurant in the West End of London by the following British actors under the direction of Poonam Brah: Rosalind Stockwell, Bobby Saigal, Jon Cartwright, Gordon Ridout and Rex Baker.

Both these readings were made possible due to the initiative of my elder daughter Namrita and the active support of my younger one Tara.

On the 2nd of October 2003, at the instance of Gita Ramchandani of Canada NewsWire, a public reading of the play, directed by Sally Jones, was held in Toronto, Canada.

The result of flying all these trial balloons was that I continued to make improvements to the text till it became production-worthy. My stenographer Mrs. Hiroo Thadhani patiently and enthusiastically typed draft after draft, and for this I thank her.

At about this point, Mrs. Rajashree Birla read the script and was kind enough to suggest that the Aditya Birla Group of companies might like to sponsor stage productions of the play in English and Hindi. I was delighted when this came about and I am most thankful to her. My appreciation extends to include the Sangit Kala Kendra and its diligent office-bearer, Mr. Lalit Daga.

My thanks also to the members of the Gandhi Smarak Nidhi, Mumbai, for their kindness and encouragement. But for all that, you would not be holding this book in your hands had it not been for the publisher, Mr. R.K. Mehra of Rupa & Co., who delighted me by agreeing to bring out this book in the shortest possible time so that it would be available in the foyer even as the play unfolded on stage. I thank and congratulate him on the efficiency of his staff which can keep pace with his sense of timeliness. In particular, I am beholden to Ms. Sanjana Roy Choudhury the editor who has now overseen the safe passage to print of three of my plays with an excellence that is evident in the very feel of the books.

Partap Sharma
12 July 2005

Sammy!" was first produced by Primetime Theatre Company, Mumbai, in both English and Hindi. Two previews were held at the Nehru Centre, Mumbai, on the 8th and 9th of July, 2005, for members of the Sangit Kala Kendra under the aegis of the Aditya Birla Group. The production opened to the public on the 30th of July, 2005, and premiered at the Tata Theatre, Mumbai, with the following cast:

MOHAN: Joy Sengupta
MAHATMA: Vijay Crishna/Ravi Dubey
KASTURBA: Neha Dubey
JAWAHARLAL NEHRU: Zafar Karachiwalla
JINNAH: Vikrant Chatturvedi
LORD IRWIN, VICEROY OF INDIA: Denzil Smith
SAROJINI NAIDU: Anu Menon
HENRY POLAK: Asif Ali Baig

The ensemble of actors played multiple roles in the drama.

The backstage crew was headed by Inaayat Ali Sami, assisted by Smita.

Director: Lillete Dubey.
Assistant Director: Ira Dubey

CAST

MAHATMA
MOHAN

and a versatile ensemble of at least three men and a woman.

The ensemble will depict:

1. Actor/Dada Abdulla/Aenoch Aasvogel/Kallenbach/O'Dwyer/Mountbatten
2. Railway Official/1st Man/Polak/ADC/Shukla/Clancy/Jinnah/Godse
3. 2nd Man/Medic/Smuts/Jawaharlal Nehru/Viceroy/Pahwa
4. Mrs. Alexander/Kasturba/Sarojini Naidu

ACT ONE

SCENE 1

To one side is a platform. On the platform: Mahatma Gandhi, staff in hand, clad in a loin-cloth. In silhouette.

MAHATMA: I am a shadow. (*As the lights come up*) The shadow of an actor.

He chuckles and turns as though to descend but the spot on him fades and he is frozen into another Mahatma attitude. Another actor enters.

ACTOR: Me too. I'm also all that. Shadow. Actor. Everything. (*Donning a padded long-coat and getting on with his preparations*) I'm part of the ensemble that will depict the other characters. That's how it is in life, isn't it? One great monumental figure (*Nods in the direction of the Mahatma)* looms out of events as though he came readymade for history but all the little fellows and fillies who may have shaped him are remembered only incidentally—as if they took life just for, and by, that brief interaction! I'm not complaining. Who am I to play Iago to his Othello? *(Using a pocket-mirror, he tidies his make-up)* I mean, there are lead roles and lead roles. Not all of us can have the big, meaty parts. Some have to live off crumbs. But that makes us versatile, adaptable. *(Sticking on a fulsome moustache and clamping a red fez cap on his head)* The great thing about being an actor is that you cross all barriers and boundaries. You break through colour, creed, kithship, kinship—the whole jing-bang shoot. You have a chance to get inside other people, feel their skin from within. You understand the conflicts and suffering of each person, *(Gives a small laugh)* even the aches in their bones. I kid you not. *(Walks with a changed, limping gait)* For instance, Dada Abdulla could feel the arthritis beginning to clutch at his right knee. *(Taps it)* Right here. And I can tell you it's bloody painful! *(He now speaks in a gruffer voice and a less sophisticated accent)* Of course, the biggest change in Dada Abdulla's life in South Africa was brought about, unexpectedly, by the juvenile behaviour of that young fellow Mohan. *(Lowering his voice as though sharing a confidentiality)* You see, I had employed him as my lawyer to iron out some trouble I was having with a cousin brother of mine. Ah, there you are, you see—I just said cousin brother. That is why I had to get myself a lawyer from India. An Indian understands these things. Here in South Africa, my company's white lawyers—like Harry Escombe—would say, "Yes, yes, your cousin." And cut out the word brother. That means Tyeb could be my cousin sister. He could be a woman. This is ridiculous. My whole approach to the civil suit would be different if I was fighting a girl. So I would say, No, no, Tyeb is a man. He is my brother, almost like a twin. We grew up together. He is a twin cousin brother. But they don't understand the agony of this family problem. Cultural differences, you see. So I had to get this johnny as we say here—this Mohandas Karamchand Gandhi all the way from India. But he gave me another kind of headache.

Mohan—a young man, in a spruce frock-coat and small, tight turban—enters in a huff as though to cross the stage. The 'Actor', now playing Dada Abdulla, limps after him.

ABDULLA: Wait! You must understand, Mohan. Mohan!
MOHAN: *(Stops)* What's there to understand, Dada Abdulla? That magistrate was picking on me. Didn't you see the way he kept staring at me? And then he asks me to remove my 'head-dress'! What's wrong with wearing a turban in court? Nobody objects in India.

ABDULLA: This is not India, Mohan. *(Shakes his head. Kindly)* Mohanbhai. *(Then pointing vigorously to the ground)* Durban, Natal, South Africa. It's different here. Why can't *you* understand that?

MOHAN: *(Thinks. Then sharply)* He didn't object to your fez.

ABDULLA: That magistrate is a fool. He took me for an Arab trader but thought that you were a mere labourer.

MOHAN: He took you for an Arab trader? But you're an Indian trader.

ABDULLA: Exactly. And it would make little difference if I was Arab or Indian—except that this *(He taps the fez)* indicates that I'm a trader. And a trader has a little more money and a little more status than a mere labourer. So he chose to pick on you.

MOHAN: How did he conclude I was a labourer? And why should he bully me for that?

ABDULLA: You see, you don't know the first thing about these people. They live by generalities and swear by race. Race signifies everything to them. Anyone who wears a fez is an Arab or a Turk. And all Arabs are traders. A brown man who doesn't wear a fez is an Indian, and every Indian is a beast of burden, a coolie. *(Indicating the fez)* This is my passport to slightly better treatment, my disguise if you wish. Of course, as a Muslim I am entitled to wear it but . . . *(Shrugs)* You have to use your wits to survive. Now take the Parsees, they call themselves Persians.

MOHAN: Which makes them—?

ABDULLA: Clerks.

MOHAN: *(Laughs)* Well, I don't want to provoke unnecessary insults. I'll wear a hat instead.

ABDULLA: In the name of Allah, no! A hat would make you an Indian Christian waiter.

MOHAN: There's no harm in being mistaken for—

ABDULLA: A Christian? Good heavens, man. Look around you. These are all Christians behaving so abominably. As for Indian Christians here, they don't associate with us. I tell you, Jesus would have had a hard time in South Africa, with his coloured skin and his desert robes. I tell you, we don't care to have anything to do with these Indian Christians. They're monkeys, flunkeys, waiters. What's so funny? Why're you laughing?

MOHAN: The way prejudice begets prejudice! We must reclaim the Indian Christians as our own. They're educated. We must stand together in the struggle.

ABDULLA: What struggle?

MOHAN: Why, the struggle against prejudice naturally.

ABDULLA: Mohan, Mohanbhai. South Africa is bigger than you. And bigger than that is the British Empire, to which we are all slaves. When we are unequal in our own country, how can we expect equal treatment in another colony?

MOHAN: Hm. You may have a point. *(Thinks, then)*

Nevertheless, I believe there's a great deal of good in the British and we can learn by their example.

ABDULLA: Mohanbhai, you may try to emulate them, but then they only give you the respect that's due to a performing chimpanzee in a zoo.

MOHAN: I'm afraid you've got a whole menagerie in me, Dada Abdulla. Something of a white elephant too.

ABDULLA: What d'you mean?

MOHAN: The fact is, I've just set up practice as a barrister. I have no experience in the courts. I get tongue-tied before an audience. I handled one case in India before coming here for yours. In that case, I stood up in court but the words wouldn't come. I had to return the fees to the client.

ABDULLA: Good heavens! And I'm suing my cousin brother for forty thousand pounds! May Allah look kindly on my misfortune.

Quick fade out.

SCENE 2

The Mahatma descends

MAHATMA: Interesting. Interesting. But, perhaps, not quite how it was. Perhaps it was much worse than we show.

Mohan enters and stands hesitantly by the wings.

MOHAN: Would you have played it differently?

MAHATMA: Of course. More diffidently. But then you are you and I am I. Though we are both the same person.

MOHAN: On stage.

MAHATMA: Indeed. And otherwise. As *all* men are one. We are together in the great divine drama of life.

MOHAN: You're sounding like Gandhi.

MAHATMA: I'm told that the actor who played Lincoln in Drinkwater's play so forgot himself in the role that he assumed it in life.

MOHAN: This is not life. We are on stage. This is a reflection of it.

MAHATMA: This is the true essence of it. Because we make no pretence, *(Shrugs)* we admit we are acting.

MOHAN: So how do you want me to go about this acting? *(Wrily)* With Brechtian 'alienation' or … *(Grimly)* the deep involvement of the Stanislavsky Method?

MAHATMA: *(Smiles)* I want you to go about it with simultaneity.

MOHAN: Simultaneity? That's a new one.

MAHATMA: It means using the ability of the mind to contain contradictions, to comprehend that something can be a dot and a wave at the same time. For an actor, it means the ability to be more than one person at the same time and to be in two places at once. It's a bit like playing Ram in the Ram-Leela. You could actually be the village's worst barber or the potter's drug-addicted, unemployed brother-in-law. You could be someone who doesn't deserve respect at all. But, while you are Ram, you'll receive veneration, people will touch your feet. Because then you *are* Ram. Though they know you are not.

MOHAN: You're sounding quite ... Vedic about it.

MAHATMA: *(Laughs)* Let's get on with it. There are lots of us, waiting to play many roles and come in on cue. On stage and in life. The wings are full of waiting souls.

MOHAN: You mean life is a charade?

MAHATMA: No, no, no, an attempt to fulfill ideals, right or wrong. If I sometimes sound like Gandhi, Gandhi was always trying to sound like himself.

MOHAN: What was he?

MAHATMA: Ah, that's the point. He spent his whole life trying to find out.

MOHAN: Are *you* trying to play my ideal?

MAHATMA: Believe it or not.

MOHAN: Hmph!

MAHATMA: I beg your pardon?

MOHAN: I said, hmph! *(Slight pause. Then)* You are not naked. *(The Mahatma chuckles)* When Churchill contemptuously called Gandhi a 'half-naked fakir', Gandhi wrote him a letter saying it was his attempt to be fully naked in both body and mind.

The Mahatma chuckles and makes as if to remove his loin-cloth. Mohan looks away.

MOHAN: Please.
MAHATMA: You see, it is you who are inhibited, bound in the strait-jacket of your times. Victorian. The charade is in the life around you. The struggle to break through is yours.
MOHAN: Life is a tragedy.
MAHATMA: A comedy of actors.
MOHAN: I can't quite see that.
MAHATMA: Not yet. Not entirely. Because you concern yourself with God.
MOHAN: God *is* Truth.
MAHATMA: *Truth* is God.
MOHAN: Anyway, you're not my ideal.
MAHATMA: *(Returning to his platform)* Not at the moment perhaps. But later.
MOHAN: I know what my ideal is. It is—
MAHATMA: *(Turns)* With your permission?

The Mahatma claps a couple of times and gestures towards the wings. Dada Abdulla enters.

MAHATMA: Not you. I want the Victorian gentleman. What's his name? Ah yes, Aenoch Aasvogel, the white South African.
ABDULLA: Right!

Dada Abdulla goes. The Mahatma returns to his level and is blotted into darkness.

SCENE 3

Aenoch Aasvogel, in a suit and top hat, enters the performing area where two benches or leather-upholstered couches have been set down facing each other like berths in a railway carriage. We hear all the sounds of a railway station.

MOHAN: *(Seeing Aasvogel)* Ah! *(Bows)* Good evening.
AASVOGEL: *(Surprised)* Hm?
MOHAN: Good evening.
AASVOGEL: *(Frowns)* Hm. *(Raises his top hat briefly)*

Aenoch Aasvogel goes past Mohan and steps into the railway carriage where he takes his seat. A stagehand dressed in black enters, hands Mohan a suitcase and three books, and retires into the wings. Mohan steps into the carriage, smiles at Aasvogel who again seems surprised and responds with a nod. Mohan places his suitcase under the berth opposite and sits down. He opens one of the books and begins reading. Aasvogel looks discomfited and drums irritatedly on the top hat in his lap. Mohan glances up and smiles. Aasvogel gets up immediately and goes out. Mohan is puzzled but returns to his book. Aasvogel comes back with a white official in uniform. They stand looking at Mohan.

OFFICIAL: Please take your seat in the van compartment. First class is for whites only.
MOHAN: But I have a first class ticket.

He takes out a ticket stub. The official looks at it quickly. Mohan stands up and smiles. The official stuffs the ticket into Mohan's pocket.

OFFICIAL: It's the van compartment for you, my man.
MOHAN: But I tell you I —
OFFICIAL: No buts. Outside!

He pushes Mohan out of the compartment, then throws his suitcase out after him. Aasvogel sits down then notices that Mohan's books are still on the berth opposite.

AASVOGEL: *(Reading the titles)* The Koran. "Unto This Last" by Ruskin. Really! These coolies are getting beyond themselves. *(Looks at the book that was open)* Good Lord! He was reading the Bible. Poor heathen!

The official salutes and leaves. The sound of the train as it starts to pull out. Aenoch Aasvogel shrugs and sits down to read the Bible. The lights fade out.

SCENE 4

The ambience turns surreal. The Mahatma and Mohan.

MAHATMA: And to think *I* ended up being called the Great Soul, Mahatma, the Mahatma! That is really what I was looking for—salvation. But life diverted me into the search for human dignity.

MOHAN: Diverted you? Is that what you call this maltreatment, this humiliation and the struggle for social justice? A diversion? A digression from your true aim?

MAHATMA: I was in search of God and stumbled upon man.

MOHAN: *(Sarcastically)* Ha! Ha! Are you making fun of my problems and a joke of me?

MAHATMA: Not at all. But I want you to see your problems in perspective. The life worth living is that of Mahavir or the Buddha. I would rather devote my energies to searching for the meaning of existence.

MOHAN: If you were a scientist, you'd probably prefer to spend your time searching for the secret of perpetual motion.

MAHATMA: That's not funny. In fact, it's a cruel remark.

MOHAN: Look, let's talk to each other honestly and openly—as actors. Don't get balled up in the character you are at this moment. Just tell me frankly: do you think that Jesus—about whom I was reading a moment ago in the Bible—got bogged down in the sociopolitical problems arising out of the fact that the Jews were being ruled by the Romans?

MAHATMA: Undoubtedly.

MOHAN: You don't think that that was his way to salvation?

MAHATMA: No. You don't have to be crucified to be saved. Nor do you need to be shot to be right.

MOHAN: So you would rather that this character had devoted his life to mere contemplation. But he was a man of action.

MAHATMA: Perforce. When necessary.

MOHAN: And it is certainly necessary now.

The light dims quickly. The MAHATMA disappears.

SCENE 5

Mohan picks up his suitcase and is walking towards the wings when Dada Abdulla, carrying a rolled-up newspaper, enters.

ABDULLA: *Salaam aleikum.* Welcome! Welcome back, Mohanbhai.

MOHAN: *Vaale kum salaam*, Dada.

ABDULLA: And how was it? How was it in the Transvaal?

MOHAN: Terrible.

ABDULLA: Did we lose the case?

MOHAN: Oh, is that what you're worrying about?

ABDULLA: What else should I be worrying about? Forty thousand pounds is not a small sum.

MOHAN: The case has been settled. Out of court.

ABDULLA: Out of court? But my forty thousand—?

MOHAN: You shall have it.

ABDULLA: All of it?

MOHAN: All. And your cousin will have the benefit of paying in easy installments.

ABDULLA: Allah be praised! But didn't I warn you my cousin brother is a most cunning man? How did you approach him?

MOHAN: Directly.

ABDULLA: Oh oh. I *told* you to avoid him. He's powerful in the community and could find ways to–

MOHAN: He was amiable.

ABDULLA: And polite and wily. Oh I know him. Was he very upset?

MOHAN: No. He saw that I had no desire to prosecute him.

ABDULLA: What? But I sent you to take him to court!

MOHAN: Quite. But why fight in court when you can agree as friends?

ABDULLA: That's most unlike a lawyer. *(Astutely)* Lawyers like to prolong cases so they can collect more fees.

MOHAN: My job was to breach a rift and not to further it. All you wanted was the money that was due to you.

ABDULLA: True, but …. You've done yourself a disservice. You should have at least got something out of Tyeb for yourself. Ah, I know what it is! You were afraid you'd have to make a speech if the case got to court.

MOHAN: *(Laughs)* Perhaps. But I did make a speech in Pretoria. To the Indian community.

ABDULLA: Oh yes, I'd quite forgotten. It was reported in the papers. I did wonder what you were doing, talking about keeping the kitchen clean or whatever it was.

MOHAN: You could say it was that. In fact, I held up the white people as an example. They are very civic minded. At the same time I asked the Indians to form an association that could protest more effectively on their behalf.

ABDULLA: And Tyeb helped you to do all this? Amazing!

MOHAN: He's president of the association.

ABDULLA: Ah! That's a stroke of genius. You're not so naïve after all. *(Slight pause)* Mohanbhai. You cannot leave us now. If you think things are terrible in the Transvaal, then read this. *(Handing him the newspaper)* On the third page. They always tuck these items away.

MOHAN: *(Glances at the item. Then)* They're depriving Indians of the right to vote.

Mohan hands the paper back thoughtfully.

ABDULLA: That's just the headline. Do you see the justification they give? *(Reads)* "The Asiatic comes of a race impregnated with an effete civilization. He thinks differently and reasons in a plane unknown to European logic—"

MOHAN: Enough. Enough. I see what you mean.

ABDULLA: I used to clip out these items and send them to friends in India as a joke. But now ... I only send the market rates. How can they imagine the way we are treated here.

MOHAN: This is a Crown Colony. Her Majesty Queen Victoria looks equally on all her subjects. The British law guarantees equal treatment.

ABDULLA: You are gullible. The most unjust thing here is the law. It twists like a snake and delivers the sting of white supremacy.

MOHAN: Then we must see that the law is not perverted. I believe in the law.

ABDULLA: What law?

The Mahatma appears. Mohan's face is turned away from Dada Abdulla. When the Mahatma speaks, it is as though Mohan had spoken.

MAHATMA: The *inner* law.

ABDULLA: *(To Mohan)* What inner law?

MAHATMA: There is a law higher than that dispensed in the courts. And when the law of the land is in conflict with that, it becomes a duty to obey the dictates of conscience.

The Mahatma disappears.

ABDULLA: Mohan, show us what to do. Bring your wife

and children from India. My company has just bought another ship. You can bring them back free on the maiden voyage.

MOHAN: I shall return with my family. For a while.

ABDULLA: Allah be praised!

MOHAN: But, Dada, don't be idle while I'm away.

ABDULLA: No, no.

MOHAN: Organize the Indians.

ABDULLA: But there are thousands of them.

MOHAN: As of now we have set up the Natal Indian Congress. *(They shake hands warmly)* Sign on every man and woman you can.

ABDULLA: Women too? *(Mohan looks quizzically at him)* Of course, of course. But surely you don't want me to go to the labourers? They're no better than slaves and have lost all spirit.

MOHAN: People always have spirit. It may simply hide somewhere waiting for a just cause and the right moment. We'll start a petition right away. And don't overlook the Christians.

ABDULLA: They're under the thumbs of the white clergymen who, in turn, take their orders from the government.

MOHAN: Sign them on. Christians, Hindus, Muslims, Jews, Parsees, agnostics, atheists, blacks, browns, the whole lot. And any white person who may wish to join.

ABDULLA: White person? But then they'll attend our meetings.

MOHAN: We have nothing to hide. Our meetings will be public and open to all. Those who sympathise may join. We are reformers, not rebels. At the end of every meeting, we shall all stand and sing "God Save the Queen".

ABDULLA: You're not serious? *(Mohan chuckles. Abdulla looks closely at him)* You're really naïve, naïve! *(He tears the newspaper and rolls it into a ball)* May Allah preserve you from the government and the lies it prints.

He throws down the ball of paper casually and is preparing to walk away. Mohan looks at the ball of paper, frowns then picks it up.

MOHAN: You know, one of the things I like about white people is that most of them are very civic minded. They keep their streets well-swept and—

ABDULLA: Oh. Ah. Yes, of course. *(He takes the ball of paper from Mohan)* Now where is that rubbish bin?

Dada Abdulla walks offstage. Mohan chuckles indulgently and follows him out. The lights fade.

SCENE 6

The lights come up to show a railing set on one side of the stage. Two Europeans stand behind the railings. They are obviously part of a scattered, hostile crowd awaiting Mohan. He is presumed to be coming through the auditorium. The sounds of a jeering crowd.

1ST MAN: It *is* him! Coming ashore in broad daylight. The cheek of the swine! *(Cups a hand round his mouth and shouts derisively)* Gandhi, go back! Go back to India!

2ND MAN: Go back, Sammy! Or we'll screw your balls off. Screw you, Sammy! Screw you!

1ST MAN: He's going to come right past us!

2ND MAN: He's headed for that house. That's Parsi Rustomji's.

1ST MAN: We'll burn it down.

2ND MAN: Ja, we'll burn it. Where's his family? I thought he'd brought his wife from India.

1ST MAN: And two children. They're all in the Parsi's house. They went ahead.

2ND MAN: He's coming. He's coming!

A lady carrying a parasol crosses quickly.

1ST MAN: 'Afternoon, Ma'am.

2ND MAN: Good afternoon, Mrs. Alexander.

MRS. ALEXANDER: Gandhi's coming down the road. They'll kill him.

2ND MAN: Yes, Ma'am.

MRS. ALEXANDER: *(Glares at him in dismay. Then)* I must phone my husband.

She goes.

1ST MAN: She's calling the police. That's the superintendent's wife.
2ND MAN: They'll be too late. *(Excitedly)* There he comes now. *(Shouts)* Yaah, knock off his turban!

Mohan stumbles in. 1st Man and 2nd Man attack him.

1ST MAN: Trample him down! Coolie bastard.
2ND MAN: Get him! Get him!
1ST MAN: Kill him! Damned coolie.
2ND MAN: Misguided, are we? We'll show you.

1st Man leans forward and slaps Mohan.

1ST MAN: *(In a hiss)* Sammy!

Mrs. Alexander walks quickly onstage. She stands beside Mohan. As the men are about to attack him again, she unfurls her parasol protectively before him. The men are dismayed. They murmur and look at each other and hesitate.

Mohan turns and seems again to shake his head slightly and chuckle. The lights dim but do not fade out. The scene freezes.

The spot on the Mahatma's platform comes on. The Mahatma descends.

MAHATMA: *(Slowly, deliberately)* Prejudice is a many-limbed, blindfolded tyrant who mocks and underestimates others and cannot see that the joke is on him. *(Walks among the frozen crowd)* These are all the slaves of prejudice. These are the many limbs of a false god. This is the violent army of the tyrant, Prejudice. They are oppressed slaves.

MOHAN: But why are they violent with me?

MAHATMA: They are afraid—of you.

MOHAN: Of me? But I wish them no harm.

MAHATMA: You would destroy the vicious god enshrined in their minds.

MOHAN: The vicious cannot be god.

MAHATMA: You see how you think?

MOHAN: God is good.

MAHATMA: May you draw strength from that notion.

MOHAN: Is it a notion?

MAHATMA: You are evolving. The universes are evolving. Perhaps God is evolving too. Perhaps the creation that is becoming defines the God that will be forever and ago. If the good succeeds, God is good; if the evil succeeds, God is evil. So my concern is not God as God may turn out to be, but the Truth. Life. As it is now.

MOHAN: The battle you describe is too much for me. I am no fighter. We have no guns to match their—

MAHATMA: Do you need guns to fight a blindfolded tyrant? The tyrant is himself a victim of his own fear.

MOHAN: We have no arms, no ammunition, no power, no authority, no skill. Only the will to fight.
MAHATMA: The spirit is enough.
MOHAN: Oh, these figures of speech!
MAHATMA: The spirit is everything.
MOHAN: In philosophy.
MAHATMA: Do you separate that from life? Then God and life are two things to you. Then spirit and action exist in two separate spheres.
MOHAN: You dictate like a Buddha embalmed in centuries but how can an ordinary person like me tackle such a vast—?
MAHATMA: These are human beings too. Remember that. Reach out to them. Take away the blindfold. They will see. They will be ashamed.
MOHAN: But how? How? How?
MAHATMA: They called you....*(Chuckles)* .... Sammy.

The Mahatma withdraws. Mohan is standing beside Mrs. Alexander again. The scene unfreezes. Mrs. Alexander looks at Mohan curiously.

MRS. ALEXANDER: Mr. Gandhi? Why're you smiling?
MOHAN: Do they know what the word 'Sammy' means?
MRS. ALEXANDER: Of course. Much of our indentured labour on the plantations comes from India, mainly from South India, and most of the names end in sammy. Ramasammy, Narayansammy. And so on.

MOHAN: The word is swami.

MRS. ALEXANDER: Surely, Mr. Gandhi, That's not important at a time like this!

MOHAN: It is. Very. Because it means master or teacher. *(To the men who are standing about watchfully)* Thank you, gentlemen. I shall endeavour to live up to that.

The men look at each other. Mrs. Alexander and Mohan leave. The lights fade.

SCENE 7

A lectern set directly facing the auditorium. Aenoch Aasvogel stands behind it, making a speech.

In proposing that we push forward legislation to control the growing influx and influence of alien populations, the herrenvolk gathered here will appreciate that I refer to more than just the Jewish problem. Suffice it to say that we propose to persuade General Smuts to consider 1) the prohibition of Jewish immigration; 2) the deletion of Yiddish as a recognized European language for immigration purposes; 3) no further naturalization of Jewish immigrants; 4) the closing of certain professions to Jews and other non-assimilable races; 5) certain other electoral restrictions. For the largest group of aliens, the Bantus, we propose the setting up of a separate Bantustan.

At present, however, the greatest threat to the policy of apartheid comes from the Asian community. It now has a leader in the quaint and extraordinary person of Mr. M.K. Gandhi. We are preparing legislation that will enable us to have Gandhi arrested. At present the law supports him. He appeals to it in the name of equality. But the new laws will crush this strange man and his strange ways. Then, to be sure, his insistence on equality will land him in jail.

The lights fade.

SCENE 8

Mohan in shirt sleeves, his coat hanging over the back of his chair, is seated at a desk to one side of the performing area. Kasturba crosses with a chamber-pot in her hand. Tears are running down her face. He watches her then explodes.

MOHAN: I won't stand this nonsense in my house! Equality must be enshrined in the heart.

KASTURBA: *(Stops)* What have I done wrong now?

MOHAN: You don't have to do it like a chore. You could take joy in the voluntary performance of an unselfish task. You could smile.

KASTURBA: Smile? *(Puts the chamber-pot down)* I am made to carry the urine of all who come here—Indian, African, European. But how can I smile when I wash the chamber-pot of an untouchable? What can wipe away that degradation? How shall I ever be purified?

MOHAN: *(Picking up the chamber-pot)* By that very act. You will raise up the untouchable and wipe away the blot on your past thought and action.

She is unconvinced but quietens. She reaches out for the chamber-pot. He looks hard at her. She realises what he wants to see. With an effort she breaks into a forced smile. He hands her the chamber-pot and turns away pleased. He checks a passage in the volume open on the table and recites a line in Sanskrit. He casually begins adjusting his clothes and knotting his necktie meticulously. Meanwhile he begins to chant a Sanskrit verse from the Bhagwad Gita. Kasturba remains standing where she is, tears welling in her eyes. She finds it difficult to keep smiling. She cannot stop herself—she bursts out crying. And sets the chamber-pot down. Mohan turns to her aghast.

MOHAN: Your stupidities will ruin me!

KASTURBA: *(Crying)* It's you who'll ruin us—the whole family. Our children are being educated to be sweepers. It wrenches at my heart to see them working with brooms. Why can't they go to a proper school?

MOHAN: Schools teach all the wrong values. I would rather teach them myself. *(Forestalling her)* Yes, even if the only time they have with me is the five-mile walk each morning to my office.

KASTURBA: There you are, you see! You don't have the time. You could engage tutors who would come to the house, or even live here.

MOHAN: Parents are the best teachers. Parental example is better than any textbook.

KASTURBA: They long for the school system.

MOHAN: Don't you influence the other boys! I know it's you who encouraged the eldest to break with me. You sent Harilal off to school in India. I won't have this, do you understand?

KASTURBA: You don't have any real love for us. You even returned the presents we were given.

MOHAN: Those presents were more than tokens. Gold watches and diamond jewellery and ... and ... they were given for my public work, not the family's. Why should you complain if we don't keep them? It's wrong to take gifts for public work. Such service is not done for material reward.

KASTURBA: Have you no sense of family? Are we to end up paupers then? When my sons marry, are their wives to receive no jewellery from me? I point out our duty and you call that temptation. You are good to the world but hard on your own flesh and blood. See how you deprived Harilal of that scholarship! He dreamed of going to England and becoming a barrister. He studied hard to prove himself. But then you said it would be wrong for someone in the family to get it even if he deserved it.

MOHAN: That would've been nepotism. I was judging the applicants. I couldn't choose my own son over others.
KASTURBA: Even when he deserved it?
MOHAN: Even so. People wouldn't understand. They'd say—
KASTURBA: Ah, so we are sacrificed to your public image!
MOHAN: That's a nasty jab! (*Grab hold of her*) Get out, woman! Get out of my house!
KASTURBA: Stop it. Be sensible. I have no one here. No relatives. Where will I go? I'm still your wife.

He hesitates and releases her. She turns to leave. Then stops and looks at him.

KASTURBA: South Africa has changed you.
MOHAN: Every man must learn and develop and change.
KASTURBA: First, it was all about Jesus, Jesus. Whatever the white men say you listen.
MOHAN: Certainly, if what they say is right. I decide for myself. I try to listen to all.
KASTURBA: Don't make your public speeches at me!
MOHAN: Think before you speak, woman!
KASTURBA: I have been thinking. Not perhaps with all those fat books like you do. And now you're learning the *Bhagwad Gita* by heart! Chanting verses every morning. Why?
MOHAN: (*Controlling himself*) Go on. Tell me why.

KASTURBA: Because you met these Theesof, these Theesofys.

MOHAN: Theosophists.

KASTURBA: Europeans trying to become Hindus!

MOHAN: Even if that were so, what's wrong? (*She is silent. Quite kindly*) You mustn't talk nonsense.

KASTURBA: (*Flaring*) Why don't you ask all of them to come and live here? You'll be better able to tell them of the glories of your religion but don't let them see how you misuse it at home.

MOHAN: I misuse it? Woman, Hinduism is rotting because of the blind actions of people like you.

KASTURBA: Ho! And you are going to save Hinduism as well, along with me and everybody and India and the whole world?

He turns away hurt. She seems to relent.

KASTURBA: Forgive me. I didn't mean to be rude. You know I'm a stupid woman. I can't even read and write. If only I could, I'd be able to follow all that you are thinking—

MOHAN: Shut up! Shut up! Every word you say wounds me to the heart. It's I who should've taught you to read and write, instead of just lusting for you.

KASTURBA: Is that lusting then? Isn't it...?

MOHAN: What?

KASTURBA: Love? (*He looks at her, then away*) I am too stupid to know. I must try and understand you.

MOHAN: Have patience with me. And, God, give me the patience too. We hurt each other too much. Even when you speak with pride of all this ... the big house, the money I'm earning, the social work I'm doing—I think, am I doing enough? How can I have a big house while people like Balasundaram struggle and starve? How can I sit in a suit discussing religion and philosophy while they suffer and are beaten bloody by their masters? Surely religion is right action. But what is the right action?

KASTURBA: Certainly not this. (*She picks up the chamber-pot*) But I'll do as you say. I'm tired of arguing with you. It exhausts me.

MOHAN: (*Bitterly*) You'll have a respite from me—

KASTURBA: (Smacks her forehead) Only when I die.

MOHAN: You won't have to wait *that* long. I'm going away for a while. I'm forming an ambulance brigade to look after the wounded in the Zulu Rebellion that is going on. You will have peace while I look after the injured at the battle-front.

She looks at him, hurt. Then turns and walks off with the chamber-pot.

The lights fade.

SCENE 9

Dusk. A log set sideways. In the distance, the sounds of gunfire. Nearer, the sound of someone singing a plaintive Zulu song. Faintly, the cries and groans of the injured and heard, interspersed with other noises of a military camp. H.S.L. Polak, a young Englishman in a rough and simple coat, with a couple of books in his hand, enters and looks about uncertainly.

POLAK: Mr. Gandhi? Where are you. Mr. Gandhi?

Mohan clad in an Ambulance Corps uniform enters followed by two Indian medical workers carrying a wounded Zulu in a stretcher.

MOHAN: Ah, Henry Polak. I'm glad to see you got here.

He signs to the stretcher-bearers tiredly to go on. They continue off-stage. Mohan looks up as though for relief then sighs and turns to Polak.

MOHAN: How did you manage to find me?
POLAK: Simple. I just asked for Sergeant Major Gandhi at the camp and they pointed this way.
MOHAN: (*Chuckles*) Well, I won't remain Sergeant Major long. The Ambulance Corps will be disbanding in a couple of days. This is no rebellion, it's a manhunt. (*Moves to the log and sits down*). The poor Zulus are

being decimated. Most of those we are treating are 'friendlies' who were shot by accident or flogged for information.

POLAK: Mr. Gandhi, I didn't mean to interrupt you in your work. (Pause) ... I hope I'm not disturbing you.

MOHAN: You couldn't disturb me half as much as my own thoughts or the sights I am seeing. Come, Henry, sit by me.

POLAK: I came to tell you that the big house in Johannesburg has been given up as you wished. Kasturba and the children are at the Phoenix settlement. I'm on my way there now.

MOHAN: Good. I have come to a decision, Henry.

POLAK: What about?

MOHAN: (With a smile) *Life*.

POLAK: That sounds like a huge decision.

MOHAN: If we are to progress beyond the pale of violence, we must purify ourselves. It is the passions that cloud our vision and lead to violence.

POLAK: Of course.

MOHAN: So you agree.

POLAK: Mr. Gandhi, ever since we met two years ago in the vegetarian restaurant, I have found no cause to disagree with you. Because what you say is always rational *and* has moral validity.

MOHAN: (*Looks away, sighs. Thoughtfully*) A great burden has been lifted from my shoulders.

Mohan seems absorbed in his own thoughts. Polak rattles on.

POLAK: I'm glad of that. In fact, I'm glad I've followed you in everything. I gave up my job and my own press to come and stay with you and run your press. I married because you suggested it. Millie had been waiting for years. She's very grateful to you. Your encouragement made me ask her to come over from England and we got married. We're so happy. So is Mr. Kallenbach and I know it's you who told him to bring a wife back with him from Europe.

MOHAN: (*Turns to him*) Henry Polak, it is our passions that make us jealous husbands. Our passions make us angry and violent with our wives. Our passions prevent us from concentrating on our work. Marching twenty to forty miles a day, with or without the wounded, through these 'solemn solitudes' I have often fallen into deep thought.

POLAK: (*Awed*) I daresay.

MOHAN: Lust or concern could have made me rush back to my wife, abandoning the sick and wounded. I know it embarrasses you that I speak like this but I have always believed it is better to be frank, otherwise the truth slips away in politenesses.

POLAK: Oh absolutely. Quite.

MOHAN: A man cannot indulge the flesh if he wishes to hone the spirit. Therefore I have decided to take a vow of celibacy, what we in India call *brahmacharya*.

POLAK: (*Handing him a little notebook and pen*) Could you ... could you write that word down for me?

MOHAN: (*Doing so*) Of course.

POLAK: Mr. Gandhi, I'm .... I'm astounded!

MOHAN: (*Hands the notebook and pen back*) It will be difficult. It will be hard. But man is man, rather than brute, because he is capable of self-restraint. The more self-restraint he exercises, the closer he moves to self-realization.

POLAK: Startling. But in line with the highest religious thinking.

MOHAN: Now, my dear Henry Polak. I don't expect you to immediately follow me on this path. Our friend Hermann Kallenbach may or may not. Our co-workers at Phoenix—Chhaganlal, Maganlal, West and others—will debate it when I put it to them and decide for themselves. I feel certain that most of them will take the vow too. A vow is a way of sealing a resolve so that it becomes unbreakable. Those of us who agree will all take it together at Phoenix.

POLAK: Have you ... consulted your wife? Kasturba may have ... other ideas or ... reservations about this.

MOHAN: You're right, Henry. This can't be a unilateral decision. (*Sighs*) Alas! I have often failed to carry conviction to Kasturba. But I think she will fall in line as she usually does.

POLAK: How ... how should one go about it? This domestic (*Looks in his notebook*) ... *brahmacharya*?

MOHAN: Stop sharing the same bed with your wife and try never to be alone with her.

Polak nods and gets up.

POLAK: Well, I'd better be on my way to Phoenix.

Mohan rises too. They shake hands. One of the uniformed Indian medical workers comes running, waving a newspaper.

MEDIC: Mohanbhai! Mohanbhai! The government has passed a bill requiring Indians to carry permits.
MOHAN: (Rising) Good heavens! That's utterly humiliating!
MEDIC: Every Indian has to register himself.
MOHAN: (Takes the newspaper) We'll resist.
MEDIC: How?
MOHAN: (Glancing at the news item) We'll find a way.
MEDIC: All your letters and petitions have not worked. We knew this was coming.
MOHAN: Henry.
POLAK: Mr. Gandhi?
MOHAN: Will you please go to Dada Abdulla of the Natal Indian Congress and ask him to organize a public meeting of all the Indians?
POLAK: All?
MOHAN: Yes, all the thousands of them. Say I shall address them. Let him fix the day and time and venue.

MEDIC: But to what purpose do you call this meeting?
MOHAN: God will show us the way.
MEDIC: Huh. Just tell us when and where and we'll be there. But, Mohanbhai, who's going to ensure that God comes too?

He makes a derisory gesture to asking. And goes. Polak shakes his head and stares after him.

POLAK: O ye of little faith!
MOHAN: Never mind, Henry. We must do what we can. And leave the rest to God.
POLAK: Indeed.
MOHAN: Do tell Hermann Kallenbach of all this. I think we have a long fight ahead of us.
POLAK: Gosh, that reminds me. He asked me to give you these books. Can you imagine, I've been here all this time and so struck by all you were saying, that I almost forgot?
MOHAN: (*Looking at the spines of the books*) Leo Tolstoy. And Henry David Thoreau. Hm. Do thank Mr. Kallenbach.

Polak nods, waves goodbye and goes. Mohan looks up and sighs.

MOHAN: O God.

The Mahatma appears.

MAHATMA: No point looking up. Unless it is for exercising your neck. Look within. The very title of the book by Tolstoy which you are holding says that. Look at it. There. What does it say?

MOHAN: (Reads as though in a daze) *"The Kingdom of God is within you."*

MAHATMA: Exactly.

MOHAN: But all I see within me at the moment is shock and hurt and horror. By this law they wish to treat all Asians as criminals. Every man, woman and child is to be fingerprinted and must carry a pass at all times.

MAHATMA: Till now it was enough that you were a lawyer. You could call on the law to aid you but now –

MOHAN: We are being treated like outlaws by the law itself!

The lights fade.

SCENE 10

A spot comes up on stage to reveal Aenoch Aasvogel at a podium.

AASVOGEL: Ladies and Gentlemen of the European Association, I call on General Jan Christian Smuts to give us an assurance that the validity of the law will be upheld. Slim Janny, please do let us have a few words from you.

He moves aside giving way to General Smuts who takes the podium.

SMUTS: None of you need have any fears on that score. As head of the government, I have today issued orders for the arrest of all Indians who refuse to register themselves, including the foolish Mr. Gandhi.

The spot goes off.

SCENE 11

Kasturba is wiping a chair with a cloth duster. Mohan enters.

KASTURBA The women and children will be deprived of the menfolk, their bread-winners. Whole families will suffer.
MOHAN: Leave me alone, woman. Let me think this through.

He moves away. She follows him.

KASTURBA: What is there to think? You are going to land everyone in jail—like common criminals.

MOHAN; (*Stops and turns to her*) That's the point. They are not common criminals.

KASTURBA: So?

MOHAN: It'll make an ass of the law.

KASTURBA: More likely it'll make asses of all of you. You'll be branded as jail-birds. You won't be allowed to practice at the bar.

MOHAN: General Smuts will understand the point we are making.

KASTURBA: Oh? He will understand! But you can't explain it to your own wife?

MOHAN: He's a barrister. Like me. He knows that a man of law will not turn frivolously to breaking it.

KASTURBA: And I am an uneducated, illiterate woman too stupid to follow your reasoning?

MOHAN: I didn't say that, Kasturi.

KASTURBA: But you meant it.

MOHAN: Kastur, for heaven's sake, let me work this out. I promise I'll make it clear as daylight to you.

KASTURBA: (*Looks at him fiercely. Then melts. Relenting*) Alright. Since you promise ... my dear. (*Shyly she gives him a peck on the cheek.*)

MOHAN: (*Drawing back*) We really mustn't be alone together. You see how these little intimacies begin? They could lead to ... anything.

KASTURBA: (*Claps her palms together and raises them to her forehead sarcastically*) *Bramhachariji*, forgive me. But just make certain you work out how you're going to earn a living if you are blacklisted from practicing at the bar.

MOHAN: Is that all you care about? Money, money, money?

KASTURBA: It's high time you thought of it too. If you can't feed yourself and your family how will you provide for the masses? Don't look so surprised. It's obvious. If you rouse them, you have to lead them; and if you lead them, you have to feed them.

She goes. Mohan sits in the chair thoughtfully. A spot shows the Mahatma on a platform. He descends.

MAHATMA: You don't have to feed them. God will provide.

MOHAN: God, God, God! We can't leave everything to God.

MAHATMA: Indeed, we can. Vast crowds followed Mahavir, Buddha, Jesus. They led men without worry. If you want to model your life on theirs then –

MOHAN: (*Jumps up*) Stop it! Stop quoting their example. I am only me. Poor little me—Mohandas Karamchand Gandhi. And Kastur has a point. Jesus did feed the multitudes. He and his disciples had to make arrangements.

MAHATMA: Of course. But it was God who provided. Loaves, fishes, basketsful of bread were gathered up later. "Care not for the morrow," he said. In the sermon on the Mount. Remember? "Behold the lilies of the field, they care not for the morrow, they toil not yet they grow." And the Gita says "Do your duty without thought of reward. Not for the fruits—"

MOHAN: Alright, alright, alright! First, before I am deprived of it, I am going to give up my legal practice. Throw myself on the mercy of God. Let Kasturi protest and cry but I am determined. (*Closing his eyes, agonised*) I am ready to put myself to the test.

MAHATMA: It is not you who is being tested but the principles expounded by Mahavir, Buddha and Jesus.

MOHAN: (*Sitting in the chair. Thoughtfully*) If there is virtue in non-violence, then there must be strength in it.

MAHATMA: Correct. If you turn the other cheek and allow yourself to be slapped again and again...

MOHAN: There must be power in the example.

MAHATMA: Is that really so? No one before this has attempted to use individual moral force as a vehicle of group action. You are trying to turn personal ethics into political possibility. You are forging a new weapon. You can change politics forever. Go now. Address them.

The Mahatma withdraws and disappears.

SCENE 12

A spot comes on. A huge cauldron set at waist level. Mohan enters, holding a piece of paper and a burning candle. He speaks as though addressing an assembly of persons.

MOHAN: Those of us who have already been issued permits should burn them now, as I do this piece of paper. (*He drops it, burning, into the cauldron. Dada Abdulla and others enter, take the candle and do the same.*) We must go calmly, happily to jail. Let no one resist arrest. Bear no ill will in your heart. Genuinely put into practice the injunction, "love thine enemy." Have no rancor, no hate. I do not think the phrase "passive resistance" adequately describes the positive strength of spirit you must have. I would rather call it "Satyagraha"—"firmness in the truth"—because we shall fight injustice non-violently by firmly asserting the truth and converting our opponents through self-suffering.

The spot goes off.

SCENE 13

Another spot comes on to show Aenoch Aasvogel and General Smuts seated in sofa chairs.

AASVOGEL: (*Laughing*) That's hilarious! I hope you're giving him a full dose of suffering through hard labour.
SMUTS: He's in for two months. That should do the trick. It'll also demoralize the stupid Europeans who have joined his movement. The two multi-racial settlements he has set up are an insult to apartheid and baaskaap.

(*Seeing an ADC approaching*) Ah, here's my man with the latest report.

The ADC enters and salutes.

ADC: Sir, the jails are filling up. Indians are flocking to be arrested. They say they want to be in prison just like Gandhi.

SMUTS: What? *Want* to be in prison?

AASVOGEL: (*Sobering*) How could these timid coolies and sammys lose their fear of incarceration?

ADC: *(Hesitantly)* I think, sir, they are moved by the example of Gandhi who has come among them and made their struggle his own.

SMUTS: 'Come among them'? Man, you are sounding half-baked and half-converted yourself. Keep a hold on your faculties.

ADC: Yes, sir.

AASVOGEL: You see, the deviousness of the Eastern mystique? It insinuates itself. *(To Smuts)* Janny, we've got to stamp it out.

SMUTS: (*To ADC*) Go on.

ADC: They … they have begun to call the prison "His Majesty's Hotel".

SMUTS: At least they have a sense of humour.

AASVOGEL: Don't they miss their home life?

ADC: Gandhi advocates celibacy, vegetarianism, fasting, denial of any enjoyment of any kind. He wants people to eat fruit and nuts. Cooked food gives too much pleasure. He recommends the prison diet and praises the rule that makes the prisoners eat their last meal before nightfall. He wants people to sleep on hard beds. He would even like them to do without the mattresses which we provide. He says he genuinely loves the prison uniform, particularly the cap. He has told his fellow-prisoners to wear it like a badge of courage even when they leave the jail. They have begun calling it the Gandhi cap.

SMUTS: Good heavens! He's making a mockery of our worst punishments.

AASVOGEL: (After a moment's thought) *Well then, let's make a mockery of him!*

The lights fade.

SCENE 14

Mohan with a newspaper in his hand, sits dejected. Kasturba is ironing clothes.

MOHAN: Do you understand what they've now done, Kasturi? When they found that they couldn't frighten us by depriving us of liberty, they've decided to wound us by denying us dignity. They've just announced that all non-Christian marriages will be deemed invalid. The state does not recognize "heathen" rites and ceremonies.

KASTURBA: Who cares what they think? They're ignorant people anyway. They don't know our traditions.

MOHAN: In addition, (*Reads from the paper*) the government will impose a three pound poll-tax on Asiatics and ban their free movement by prohibiting entry into the Transvaal. (*Putting the paper aside*) I'm at my wit's end. I don't know what to do.

KASTURBA: Have your orange juice, that's what you should do. It'll clear your brain. I've got it ready in the kitchen.

MOHAN: I'm astounded. You don't appreciate the enormity of this.

She goes. The Mahatma appears.

MAHATMA: They say, every time a door closes, a thousand others open.

MOHAN: I don't see that. I'm at a dead end. Even Kasturba doesn't realize what I'm talking about.

MAHATMA: Injustice is best fought by those most affected by it.

MOHAN: But the new regulations affect women and their babies.

MAHATMA: Help the women to understand the implications. Then let them, along with their babies, fight non-violently for their rights.

MOHAN: What? Women and *babies?*

MAHATMA: Why not? Let babies and children and women lead the protest.

MOHAN: But that's unheard of.
MAHATMA: Let them hear of it now.

The Mahatma chuckles and disappears.

MOHAN: (*Shouts*) Kastur! Come here. Quick.

Kasturba enters with a glass of orange juice.

KASTURBA: I was just bringing it. I knew you'd become impatient for it. I had it ready.
MOHAN: (*Taking it*) Thank you, thank you. Now listen. Did you know we've been living in sin all these years? You're not my wife, you're just my kept woman.
KASTURBA: (*Smacks her forehead*) *Hey Bhagwan!* What crass kind of joking is that?
MOHAN: I'm not joking. It's the new law. According to it, our children are illegitimate and will be treated as bastards.
KASTURBA: Oh! This is stupid, evil, ridiculous!
MOHAN: I knew you would think so. And I want you to do something about it.
KASTURBA: Me? What can I do?
MOHAN: Lead the protest with other women and children.
KASTURBA: You want me to lead? You want women and children to come out on the street?
MOHAN: Yes, yes. The men will follow, of course. Court arrest. So will the men. We shall march slowly and

peacefully from Natal into Transvaal without permits. Altogether we shall be about two thousand marchers.

KASTURBA: (*Sinking down in the chair*) Now it is I who am astounded. You come up with the strangest ideas!

Mohan smiles and gives her a kiss on the forehead. The lights fade.

SCENE 15

General Smuts and Aenoch Aasvogel in conversation over a glass of sherry.

SMUTS: We've had Gandhi arrested three times in four days yet the march continues even without him. We need to find someone who has influence over him. Tell me, Aenoch, who does he consult? Who guides him?

AASVOGEL: They say he gets it all from … (*A bitter laugh*) … his "inner voice".

SMUTS: How can I get a hold on that?

AASVOGEL: Maybe you should get yourself an inner voice too. His seems to come up with a lot of strategies and tactics. It certainly isn't just his conscience he consults.

SMUTS: What is unique is that he really has made each person his own leader. Arresting him has not disheartened the others. They keep marching. We keep arresting the ones in front. The others keep marching.

One young woman lost her baby in a flooded river which they forded and she kept walking. Carrying her grief instead of her child. Another's son died. She had him cremated and continued on the march. We're facing something that drives people from within. It's awesome.

AASVOGEL: We could turn them into cannon-fodder if…

SMUTS: If what?

AASVOGEL: They rioted. Killed a European.

SMUTS: No, no, no.

AASVOGEL: Suppose they hurt a European woman? Even chased her down the road? Frightened her?

SMUTS: They won't. Damn it, they won't! They won't riot. They won't lose their firmness in peace or whatever they call it. It's … it's most distressing.

The lights go off.

SCENE 16

General Smuts standing by a table, talking to his ADC. Smuts is in a furious mood. He brings his baton down hard on the table.

SMUTS: Damn it! What do you mean the Indians are boycotting the commission? It's been set up to look into their grievances. I'm extending a hand to them! They can't ignore my offer.

ADC: They say they'd like the commission to have an Indian on it or, at any rate, a representative they select.

SMUTS: Impossible! They can't dictate terms to us. Gandhi is now trying to rub my nose in the dirt. We'll get that Englishman what's-his-name? The fellow sent out by the viceroy of India to help us resolve these problems.

ADC: Sir Benjamin Robertson.

SMUTS: That's right. Lord Hardinge's man can persuade the Indians.

ADC: It seems, sir, that nobody can persuade Mr. Gandhi. (*Holding out a document*) Here's a copy of a long cable he has just sent to the man he calls his mentor in India.

SMUTS: Ah, you mean Gokhale. Good. (*Taking the cable*) I knew both Gokhale and Hardinge would tell Gandhi to co-operate with us. Now, at last, we can settle this whole mess.

ADC: I'm afraid, sir, Mr. Gandhi politely disagrees with him, even at the cost of further affecting Mr. Gokhale's already poor health.

SMUTS: (*Reading the cable and striking the table with his baton*) Damn it! Damn it! Damn it!

ADC: Shall I let him in, sir?

SMUTS: Who?

ADC: Mr. Gandhi, sir. He's waiting outside to see you. *He gave me that copy of his cable to Gokhale. He wanted you to see it. He says he believes in total openness in his dealings.*

Smuts stares at his ADC. A slight pause. Smut seems to take charge of himself.
SMUTS: Show him in.

The ADC goes. Smuts strikes the table with his baton.

SMUTS: Damn it!

Smuts tucks the baton under his arm, adjusts his clothes and composes himself. Mohan is led in. His head is clean-shaven. He is wearing a faded white kurta and "lungi" like a South Indian labourer. He is carrying a brown package. The ADC withdraws.

SMUTS: (*Smiling*) Hello, Mr. Gandhi. How nice to see you again. (*The smile fades*) Good God! What have you done to yourself?
MOHAN: I beg your pardon, General Smuts?
SMUTS: Where's your suit, man? You always came here dressed in a suit. And your hair? What's happened to it?
MOHAN: I was always prone to baldness.
SMUTS: But, no, no, you've shaved your head. Like one of those Hindoo labourers. And you're dressed like one of them.
MOHAN: Exactly. To show solidarity with their suffering.
SMUTS: You are rubbing salt into my wounds, Mr. Gandhi.
MOHAN: *Your* wounds? No one has struck you or shot

at you as your mounted military police have done with the poor indentured labourers.

SMUTS: But you have inflicted the deeper injury on me by your peacefulness.

MOHAN: Ah. You are beginning to see that?

SMUTS: (*Sighs*) It has been distressing me for some time.

MOHAN: Oh? I did not mean to cause you distress.

Smuts waves Mohan towards a chair and sits down.

SMUTS: The problem is that you are a man of peace. Had you been otherwise, I would have dealt with you... otherwise. But how can I go on harassing a peaceful man.

MOHAN: (*Sympathetically*) How can you kill the voluntarily dead?

SMUTS: (*In frustration*) There's no joy in fighting a walking corpse!

MOHAN: (*Understandingly*) There is no pleasure in hanging someone who welcomes death.

SMUTS: My soldiers want to see some reaction, some resistance from your lot.

MOHAN: If the lion, on seeing a Great Hunter approach, lay down on his back and put his paws in the air, the hunter would find nothing great in killing the playful and friendly lion. Great Hunters would give up lion hunting if the lion took to non-resistance.

Smuts gets up and walks up and down briskly. Then he stops.

SMUTS: Mr. Gandhi, there is no joy for me in this hunt.
MOHAN: You concede all our demands?
SMUTS: I do. Because I see they are just.
MOHAN: (*Placing a sheet of paper on the table.*) The five points are listed there. One, repeal of the £3 tax; two, legalization of marriages celebrated according to the rites of Hinduism, Islam etc; three, allow the entry of educated Indians into —
SMUTS: Yes, yes, yes. I'm well aware of all the points.

He walks to the table and punches a bell. The ADC enters.

ADC: Sir?
SMUTS: (*Handing him the paper*) Place this before the commission for its approval.
ADC: (*After a quick glance at the contents*) Approval, sir?
SMUTS: You heard me. Approval. Complete and absolute.
ADC: (*Salutes*) Aye, aye, sir. (*Going thoughtfully. Stops. Turns*) It's been a long battle for all concerned. Allow me, sir, to be the first to congratulate you on arriving at a settlement to the vexed problem.
SMUTS: Thank you.
ADC: Mr. Gandhi, congratulations on achieving an approval so complete and abject.
MOHAN: Not abject. Absolute.
ADC: Of course, that's what I meant.

MOHAN: In satyagraha, we do not seek to demolish or destroy the opponent but to win him over to our view.

SMUTS: (*Smiles*) And I am won over completely.

MOHAN: General Smuts, with this task done, I shall probably leave for India.

SMUTS: I can't say that won't be a relief for us.

MOHAN: My plan is to go first to England to seek the advice of my mentor Mr. Gokhale who is in Europe for medical treatment. His experience will guide my actions in India. For, in India, still greater tasks await me.

SMUTS: I dread to think of the fate of any politician or administrator who might dare oppose you.

MOHAN: (*Smiles*) I am only a channel for the truth. General Smuts, in all these years of confrontation, we have come to know each other quite well. As a token of my esteem, I would like to present you a sample of my own handiwork. (*Mohan holds out the package. General Smuts hesitates and looks at this ADC*) Don't worry. It's not a bomb. I don't believe in violence.

General Smuts takes it and quickly opens it. The ADC watches fascinated.

SMUTS: Sandals!

MOHAN: I made them for you myself. In prison. It was a wonderful learning opportunity.

He joins his palms in namaste. Then goes.

The ADC goes up and touches the sandals.

ADC: (*Softly*) It's good leather.

SMUTS: (*Moved*) But I am not worthy to stand in the shoes of so great a man.

Lights off.

SCENE 17

Mid-day. An unfurnished room in London. Mohan is discovered seated on a grey blanket that has been spread on a portion of the floor. He is eating something with a wooden spoon from a wooden bowl. Around him are some old tins.

A young Indian lady, Sarojini Naidu, of about thirty-five years of age, knocks on the door that is ajar and enters. She is well-bred, confident and sophisticated. She has a letter in her hand, which she has obviously been consulting for the address which she has now located. She surveys the scene, aghast, amazed, disbelieving.

SAROJINI: Oh my ... good heavens! You can't be ... Are you ... ?
MOHAN: Mohandas Karamchand Gandhi.

SAROJINI: (*Bursts into laughter*) I don't believe this! You're the great Gandhi, vanquisher of General Smuts! But you're a little man, a wee brown Mickey Mouse of a man!

He begins laughing.

MOHAN: And you must be the very dramatic, very poetic, very voluble Mrs. Sarojini Naidul.

SAROJINI: So Mr. Gokhale sent you a letter too?

MOHAN: (*Nods*) Your reputation precedes you. Who hasn't heard of the nightingale of India?

SAROJINI: Some people pronounce it differently and call me the naughty girl of India. (*He laughs*) I'm glad you have a sense of humour. I couldn't have borne it if you were one of those dull holy types. Mr. Gokhale sends his apologies. He's stuck in Paris. He's trying to get here but the war has closed all frontiers and it's difficult.

MOHAN: Do sit down and join me in a bit of lunch.

SAROJINI: (*Looking around*) But there's nothing to sit on. No furniture. Why didn't you take a furnished room?

MOHAN: This suffices. We have my prison blanket to sit on.

SAROJINI: Prison blanket? And I daresay that wooden spoon and bowl are souvenirs of prison too?

MOHAN: They're simple and sturdy and perfectly adequate.

SAROJINI: Hm. I can see you need some poetry in your life. (*Opens her handbag and takes out two slim volumes*) By way of a beginning may I present you two of my books of poems? I brought them thinking you might enjoy reading them.

MOHAN: I'm sure I will.

Sarojini sits down quickly, places the books beside him, then takes the bowl from him, looks at the contents with dismay and hands it back.

SAROJINI: What is this uncooked mess you're eating?
MOHAN: Squashed tomatoes, ground-nuts and dried bananas mixed together in olive oil.
SAROJINI: Ugh. What an awful concoction!
MOHAN: My wife would agree with that. She's gone out in search of what she calls "a proper lunch". However, if you'd care to join me—
SAROJINI: No, thank you.

She gets up and walks about, looking around. He continues eating.

SAROJINI: You've taken some kind of vow of poverty, haven't you? Gokhale was telling me.
MOHAN: Non-possession.

SAROJINI: Look, if you're short of funds, I could lend you something. Or take you out for a meal.

MOHAN: Mrs. Naidu, during the years I studied here, I became fully acquainted with the so-called "civilized" penchant for elaborate meals conducted with great éclat. Many courses, each with its own wine, buttressed on either side by sherry, port and sometimes champagne, the whole proceeding drawn out beautifully till a soon is tapped on glass and the rite of formal speeches rounds off the ritual. Members of the Inner Temple who are called to the bar were often referred to as "dinner barristers" because we had to attend so many of twenty-four dinners per term and there were twelve terms. So we emerged quite able, at least, to dine splendidly.

SAROJINI: But?

MOHAN: No but. I just prefer this.

SAROJINI: Ah.

She walks about. He continues eating. There is an awkward silence.

MOHAN: (*After a while*) You have children, Mrs. Naidu?

SAROJINI: And a husband.

MOHAN: Naturally.

SAROJINI: Not necessarily. Some people have the one without the other.

MOHAN: How many?

SAROJINI: Husbands?
MOHAN: (*Smiles*) No. Children.

SAROJINI: Four.
MOHAN: (*While eating*) A good relationship?
SAROJINI: With my husband?
MOHAN: No, no. I meant, with the children.
SAROJINI: Well, they pummel me all over and climb into my bed at eight in the morning. They fight over portions of me as though conquering a battleground.
MOHAN: So they are awake well before you?
SAROJINI: Of course. Little children always wake early.
MOHAN: But you don't get up till eight?
SAROJINI: Not a minute before. I'm their Mummy, not their Nanny. Look here, Mr. Gandhi, if you're implying that a good mother has to be up early before her children—?
MOHAN: No, no. No such thing. I can quite picture the scene. The children flocking round you and scrambling into the softness of motherly affection. What could be more maternal? Surely there could be no greater love than this.
SAROJINI: (*Picking up a wooden spoon*) Mr. Gandhi, you seem simple but I suspect you are a very clever man. In addition to that, I'm sure you're a very great man. Yet I can also see that you are not a great cook. Nevertheless, I shall join you in whatever public service tasks you may wish to share with me, including the

awful prospect of downing some of that frugal, ascetic, uninspiring stuff.

She dips her spoon into his bowl.

MOHAN: That is exactly the idea. Food should inspire you to nothing. Would you like to use a clean bowl?

SAROJINI: This one is not unclean to me. It is your bowl. I would like to share it. (*Taking another spoonful*) If you were an untouchable, this would be breaking caste barriers. It would be more radical than what is called "inter-dining". (Eats) In Hyderabad where I have my home, the Muslims often eat together out of the same bowl. I like that. It means everyone is equal. Now, if I were a Muslim and we ate together like this, it would help bring about Hindu-Muslim unity. I know you are as keen on that as I am.

MOHAN: Indeed. (*Smiles*)

SAROJINI: But why are you smiling? (*He seems to hesitate*) Tell me truthfully.

MOHAN: I am always truthful.

SAROJINI: Then tell me what you were thinking just now.

MOHAN: That you really are a songbird. You speechify and warble with words even while eating. You are just one person but you've brought a great flurry and noise with you that fills this room.

SAROJINI: I should be offended. But I know you are sincere. However, what you remark on as though it were a fault in me is, in fact, my forté. Words give me wings and, when I fly, I carry people with me.

MOHAN: A veritable garuda. Yes, you can help fly India to freedom.

SAROJINI:(*Thrilled*) Freedom? For India? Is that your aim?

MOHAN: I would settle for dominion status like Canada or Australia. But, if that is not forthcoming, then complete freedom.

SAROJINI: But how?

MOHAN: Through satyagraha.

SAROJINI: (*Laughs and moves away*) I know you succeeded in South Africa. But the British Empire circles the globe. The sun never sets on it. It is the strongest, greatest empire the world has ever known.

MOHAN: (*Gently*) The soul force of satyagraha is the strongest, greatest weapon the world has ever known.

She looks at him silently for a few seconds. Then.

SAROJINI: Mr. Gandhi, in a couple of days I intend to hold a grand public reception in your honour where, before a large gathering of Indian and British persons, I would like to garland you. It will be a privilege to hear you address the gathering.

MOHAN: Thank you. I would welcome an opportunity to make my views known, especially to Indians resident in Great Britain and Ireland.

SAROJINI: You will say a few words then? Oh I'm so

delighted. You can step forward on English soil and unfurl the banner of India's freedom.

MOHAN: (*Getting up*) Oh no, no, Mrs. Naidu. I would not like to do anything as grandiose as that. The British people are in difficulty at present. There is a war on. (*Calmly, while putting the dishes away*) I would not like to take advantage of the government's preoccupation. This is Britain's hour of need. We must render it assistance. I would like to call upon all Indians, and people of other nationalities residing in Britain, to do their bit towards the war effort. Those who live here and enjoy the benefits of this system must volunteer to serve in the armed forces.

SAROJINI: The armed forces? But, Mr. Gandhi, isn't that contrary to your own—?

MOHAN: (*Smiles understandingly*) If they are adherents of non-violence then they can join the medical corps which I propose to set up. But they cannot escape their clear duty to do something helpful at this juncture.

SAROJINI: You have a point, of course, in that cowards must not take shelter in the guise of non-violence –

MOHAN: Do you think we could get together about a hundred Indians to form an ambulance corps?

SAROJINI: I ... I shall try. But I must confess, Mr. Gandhi, you puzzle and astound me.

MOHAN: Lord Crewe seemed startled too when I made the offer soon after arrival. He was sure nobody would believe it of me. So I promised to send it to him in writing, and that is what I shall now do. What're you waiting for? (*Claps his hands quickly three times as though to wake her up*) Go on, get to work.

SAROJINI: (*Going, stops*) No wonder Gokhale says that you have the capacity to mould heroes out of common clay.

MOHAN: (*Chuckles*) And heroines. I find women often perform better than men under conditions of stress.

SAROJINI: I'm a member of the Lyceum Club. I'm sure the ladies there would be very happy to do anything to—

MOHAN: Excellent. They can cut patterns of cloth for uniforms. We'll need about a hundred and fifty to start with. The men can do the stitching and sewing themselves. (*Picking up a pad and pen*) Let me know how you've progressed by tomorrow morning.

Sarojini's jaw drops. Her mouth hangs open. Her eyes widen. She nods a couple of times. He looks at her quizzically.

MOHAN: Yes?

SAROJINI: (*Shakes her head*) I've never been struck speechless before.

He laughs and settles down crosslegged on the blanket to write, holding the pad in one hand and the pen in the other.

MOHAN: Off you go then.

SAROJINI:: Thank you.
MOHAN: For what?
SAROJINI: For making me feel so useful.

She goes. He begins writing.

MOHAN: (*Softly*) Dear Lord Crewe...

The lights fade.

SCENE 18

The lights come up again almost immediately. Mohan has finished the letter and is folding it into an envelope. Behind him the Mahatma appears.

MAHATMA: Ego, ego, ego. Vanity, vanity, vanity.
MOHAN: (*Without turning round*) No, no, no.
MAHATMA: She flattered you, called you great. A public reception in your honour! The Gita says, "Not for the fruits of your action but do the action for itself." Here you are, plucking the fruits of your victory in South Africa. You will be garlanded, praised, extolled.
MOHAN: I have things to say, aims to accomplish.
MAHATMA: You made the offer to Lord Crewe in haste. You didn't consider, you didn't consult.
MOHAN: Why should I always consult you?

MAHATMA: Ah ha, rebelling against your own conscience? A true anarchist, torn apart within yourself.
MOHAN: My mind is clear. This letter must go to him. I am doing what I must.

Mohan has not turned to face the Mahatma. He closes the envelope and writes the address.

MAHATMA: Lord Crewe thanked you for tendering service to the Empire at this critical hour. (*Mohan sits up thoughtfully*) You want to make the British feel grateful.
MOHAN: (*Gets up*) I'm going. To post this letter. Or deliver it, if necessary.
MAHATMA: Wait!

Mohan still does not look at the Mahatma. It is obvious he is looking within.

MOHAN: (*Thoughtfully*) Is conscience a social phenomenon? Or is it innate in man, a gift of nature, a genetic configuration, an insistence of the spirit, the voice of Truth, a reflection of God?
MAHATMA: Go on. You'll soon find a way to discredit my existence and then ignore me. (*He moves right up to Mohan*) What are you hoping for? Another medal as in South Africa? Perhaps even a title? A knighthood. Sir Mohandas K. Gandhi, Servant of Empire. Or a baronetcy? Something even the children can inherit.

Mohan is anguished and about to fling the pad and pen down.

MOHAN: Shut up!

MAHATMA: (*Cautioningly*) Un unh! Self control. Ahimsa. Non-violence. On Tolstoy Farm, you once lost your temper and struck a mischievous boy.

MOHAN: It taught him a lesson.

MOHAN: Ah. So violence has its uses?

Mohan puts the pad and pen away. The letter goes into a pocket.

MOHAN: But participation in war can never be consistent with ahimsa.

MAHATMA: You acknowledge that?

MOHAN: Yes! And I admit that I am hoping to improve my status and that of my people through the British Empire.

MAHATMA: (*Sarcastic*) You mean, when the British government sees that you can't be ordered like a slave but you will voluntarily serve, you may in recompense be given greater freedom, even dominion status?

MOHAN: That's right. The same distinction I made in South Africa between voluntary registration and coerced registration.

MAHATMA: For which subtle distinction you almost got killed by that pathan Mir Alam.

MOHAN: But I was hoping that Smuts would see the point.

MAHATMA: (*Laughs*) Your naïveté and gullibility are so ingrained that you've turned them into high philosophy!

MOHAN: Go on. Make me hate myself. Rob me of my confidence. Didn't the poet say, "Thus conscience doth make cowards of us all"? I am what I am and must face that.

MAHATMA: Then face me. Face the facts.

Mohan turns to face the Mahatma.

MOHAN: I am prepared to confess all my failings to the whole world and I shall at the first opportunity.

MAHATMA: What an indulgence!

MOHAN: Yes, yes, whip me, flagellate me, make me suffer.

MAHATMA: Masochist!

MOHAN: I shall emerge purer for being drenched in the fountain of pain.

MAHATMA: You *are* a coward. As a child you were afraid of ghosts, apparitions, things in the dark. So you've made fearlessness part of your creed.

MOHAN: If a man is lame, may he not walk with a stick? A vow helps.

MAHATMA: You were disgusted by the fact that your father was so highly sexed that he had to get himself four wives. Your mother Putlibai was twenty-five years younger than him. What a lech he was! You yourself enjoyed sex so much that you were lost in the pleasure of erotic contortions with Kasturi, caught up in the ecstatic mists of lust, unmindful that your father was dying in the next room and calling out to you.

MOHAN: Oh oh ... that is my eternal shame!

MAHATMA: The guilt rises up to you more threatening than any ghost.

MOHAN: (*Shaking his head*) I can never face him. (*Anguished*) O father!

MAHATMA: So you blame, not yourself, but your desire. You do not say there is a time and place for it; you chose the wrong time and place.

MOHAN: It offends me. I cut if off. I prefer *brahmacharya*.

MAHATMA: You were a thief. As a child, you stole money for cigarettes.

MOHAN: "Thou shalt not steal," the Bible says.

MAHATMA: Non-stealing is now one of your eleven vows. You wanted to be wealthy –

MOHAN: I urge non-possession. Better to have nothing. No temptation for thieves. No lure for robbers. No distraction from the path of purity.

MAHATMA: You have been hiding yourself from yourself.

MOHAN: I shall state it all, write it all, publish it. "The truth shall set thee free."

MAHATMA: And now this! Polak and others will be horrified when they hear of it. You are not even taking the path of the conscientious objector and refraining from participation. You are helping in the pursuit of war.

MOHAN: I am doing it merely as my duty to the Empire.

MAHATMA: The truth of the matter is staring you in the face but you will not look at it. You know why you are setting up a medical corps—not for the first time but the third time—and again in a time of war?

MOHAN: Tell me.

MAHATMA: Because you always wanted to be a doctor. Not with your mud-packs and potions but a proper doctor.

MOHAN: I love nursing the sick, healing the wounded. Yes, I wanted to be a doctor.

MAHATMA: But the family was against it. You remember the words—?

MOHAN: (*Nods*) "We Vaishnavas should have nothing to do with dissection of dead bodies."

MAHATMA: So you couldn't have become a qualified doctor. But war provides a break with normalcy. A man can help by doing what he always wanted to do. But after the war what will you do?

MOHAN: I shall travel silently in India for a year as Gokhale has suggested. Then I shall speak out truthfully—without fear or favour. But right now, I have a letter to post.

He starts to leave. The Mahatma disappears. The lights fade.

SAROJ: *(involuntarily)* That O'Dwyer is a stupid man! What else could he expect? If you shoot at the innocent, the _____ bound to retaliate. It shows the people's _____ now the whole nation will rise up in anger—

MOTHER: _____ no, no! You are wrong to be pleased. It's a sh_____ May God show us the way to atone for the sins _____ countrymen, and may God help us to persuade those who oppose us to see our point of view. _____ one of these deaths diminishes us. Revenge is _____ an eye for an eye" will only leave the whole world _____

_____ _____ _____ *(standing, the group rises with him.)*

MOTHER: _____ is no excuse. We must first curb our own _____ violence and turn it into love that cares for _____ You are a poet. Is there a poem, perhaps, _____ that would hold good for our situation now?

_____

_____ in _____ _____
_____ fire and _____ supplies
_____ upper themes their sky
_____ your _____ and lava _____
Then they will return with storm
To the place from which they came,
_____ soaked all the blood it had shed _____

ACT ONE, Sc. 3
Mohan learns the meaning of apartheid in South Africa.

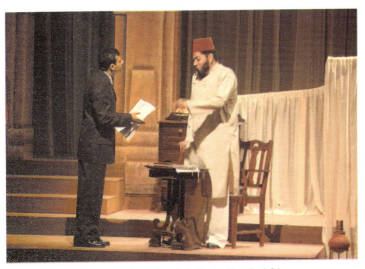

Mohan and Dada Abdulla in South Africa
ACT ONE, Sc. 5
Dada Abdulla: "The most unjust thing here is the law."

ACT ONE, Sc. 6.
"Go back, Sammy! Go back to India."

ACT ONE, Sc. 8.
"I won't stand this nonsense in my house! Equality must be enshrined in the heart."

ACT ONE, Sc. 9.
Henry Polak hears from Sergeant Major Gandhi of the Ambulance Corps that he has decided to take a vow of celibacy.

Mohan and the Mahatma in debate.

ACT ONE, Sc. 12.
M. K. Gandhi burns his permit.

ACT ONE, Sc. 13.
"Sir, the jails are filling up. Indians are flocking to be arrested. They say they want to be in prison just like Gandhi."

ACT ONE, Sc. 13
Aasvogel: "Well then, let's make a mockery of him!"

ACT ONE, Sc. 13
Gen. Smuts: "Good heavens! He's making a mockery of our worst punishments."

ACT ONE, Sc. 14
"The new marriage regulations affect women and their babies....
Let babies and children and women lead the protest."

ACT TWO, Sc. 2.
Jawaharlal and Sarojini discuss this 'phenomenon' called Gandhi.

ACT TWO, Sc. 4
Sarojini: "Bapu, Bapu! Terrible news from Punjab. Terrible news!"

Jinnah: "What alternative can there be?"

ACT TWO, Sc. 23
Mountbatten: "Very well then, Partition it shall be.
Divide your assets."

ACT TWO

SCENE 1

A spot comes on to show Rajkumar Shukla, a poor peasant from Bihar, waiting. He has a rolled-up sheet of paper in his hand. He seems to be memorising some lines. He checks the paper and begins to spout the lines.

SHUKLA: Gandhiji. Ever since you arrived in India I have been hearing of your concern for the poor. What a blunt speech you made at the opening of the Benares Hindu University! It upset many people but it gave us hope. Please come to our assistance.

Mohan comes past.

SHUKLA: Gandhiji.
MOHAN: What is it?

SHUKLA: (*Going blank*) Umm bum baaa. Ah ah ah… (*Thrusts the paper at him*)

MOHAN: (*Glances at paper*) Thank you. Now, if you'll excuse me. I'm in a bit of a hurry. (*Starts to leave*)

SHUKLA: Wait, wait! Please. I've come to Lucknow all the way from Champaran only to meet you. I knew you'd be here to attend the meetings of the Indian National Congress. Thousands of peasants like me are suffering because we are forced to grow indigo and supply it to the British planters.

MOHAN: What is indigo? Where is Champaran?

SHUKLA: Come with me. We'll go by train. Let me show you our suffering.

MOHAN: I … I have no time now. What is indigo?

SHUKLA: It is a plant used for making a vegetable dye. Under the "tinkathia" system, we are forced to grow it on a part of our land no matter what the difficulty. It causes a lot of hardship. Even if we are starving, we have to grow the indigo.

MOHAN: Get someone to move a resolution in Congress expressing sympathy.

SHUKLA: Please. Would you?

MOHAN: I have to go to Kanpur.

The spot goes off. Another spot comes on. Mohan enters the light. At the same time Shukla enters the spot from another side.

SHUKLA: I've come to Kanpur to request you to kindly—
MOHAN: Sorry. I have to go to my Ashram in Ahmedabad.

The spot goes off. Another comes on elsewhere. Mohan enters it, followed by Shukla.

SHUKLA: Excuse me, Gandhiji, I've come to your ashram to beg you to—
MOHAN: My schedule's very tight these days.
SHUKLA: I know. I'm told you're expected to go soon to Calcutta to visit someone called Bhupen Babu.
MOHAN: (*Puzzled*) That's right.
SHUKLA: That's perfect.
MOHAN: For what?
SHUKLA: Your trip to Champaran.
MOHAN: But—

The spot goes off. Another comes on. Mohan enters from one side, Rajkumar Shukla from the other.

SHUKLA: Welcome to Calcutta!
MOHAN: What are you doing here, in Bhupen Babu's house?
SHUKLA: I told them we would be travelling together and they let me stay.
MOHAN: What audacity! (*Sighs*) Alright. How do we get to Champaran?
SHUKLA: From Calcutta we go to Patna, from Patna to

Muzaffarpur, from Muzzaffarpur to Motihari in Tirhut, and from there to Bettiah and from Bettiah to my place in Champaran.

MOHAN: (*Laughs*) Very well then. Show me the way.

SHUKLA: I hope you don't mind.

MOHAN: How can I mind when you are so persistent and have so much faith in my ability to help you?

SHUKLA: I mean, I hope you don't mind that we shall be travelling by train and bullock-cart and, finally, by elephant.

Mohan looks stunned then bursts out laughing. The lights fade.

SCENE 2

Early morning. A sofa set. Sarojini Naidu, with a bundle of files and documents in her lap, is seated in one of the chairs. Across from her, perched on the arm of a sofa is Jawaharlal Nehru, thirty years old, dressed in riding breeches and carrying a crop in one hand.

JAWAHAR: Amazing. Absolutely amazing. He's sweeping through the countryside like a forest fire.

SAROJINI: Not without reason, Jawahar. He works hard. (*Patting the files*) These are "Case studies of the success of satyagraha." I've compiled them for your father. Motilalji wants Congress to understand how carefully

Gandhi works. It's not all airy-fairy high-heaven talk. In Champaran alone *he recorded eight thousand statements.*

JAWAHAR: Eight thousand! Good heavens! As a barrister myself, I know what that means. (*Moves to a silver box of cigarettes*) So he's both organized and other-worldly. What a combination! I'm sorry my father's keeping you waiting. Shall I go and see what's holding him—?

SAROJINI: No, no, please. *I'm* early.

JAWAHAR: Well, I'm jolly glad I got back from my ride when I did. It's given me a chance to have a chat with you and I'm so dying to know more about this phenomenon.

SAROJINI: Phenomenon?

JAWAHAR: Gandhi.

SAROJINI: Ah.

Jawahar proffers the box of cigarettes. She declines. He takes one out for himself. During the course of the conversation he sticks the cigarette in a filter-holder and lights up.

JAWAHAR: I'm trying to decide whether I should argue with him or agree with him. You will join us for breakfast, won't you?

SAROJINI: Thank you, I've already eaten. I used to get up lazily by eight and eat by nine but Gandhiji has changed all that. One snide remark from him and I'm a different creature. That's his forté, changing people.

JAWAHAR: I'd better watch out then.

SAROJINI: Oh, he'll change you. Whether you agree with him or not. I'm told that young English officers newly arrived in India are warned, "Stay away from Gandhi or he'll get you!"

JAWAHAR: Well, he's certainly got the peasants of India. They call out to him as Bapu or father. And the poet Rabindranath Tagore has hailed him as a Mahatma.

SAROJINI: (*Smiles*) Mahatma Gandhi. You know, the other day a friend said to me, "It is only India that knows how to honour greatness in rags." It is a homage that emperors cannot buy.

The lights fade.

SCENE 3

The sound of twenty thousand people thundering "Mahatma Gandhi ki jai!" and "Vict-o-r-y to Mahatma Gandhi!" "Bharat mata zindabad!" "Long live Mother India."

Mohan, in a white dhoti and sandals, shaven-headed without the 'shendi' or tuft of hair at the back of the skull, wrapped in a sheet but otherwise bare-bodied from the waist up, enters. He is bespectacled and walks with a staff in hand as many peasants do.

MOHAN: (*Waves to an invisible crowd for silence*) During the four years of the war, I have been a recruiting agent for the British. I have trudged the countryside asking India to offer all her able-bodied sons as a sacrifice towards the defence of the Empire. I had expected that, in appreciation of the millions of lives readily given to protect Britain, India would, on the successful conclusion of the war, be given dominion status. No such thing has happened. We had expected that when our troops returned from the front, there would be a relaxation of the draconian Defence of India rules. But, instead, the harsh wartime measures are being continued and repression reinforced by the newly-passed Rowlatt Act. Indians will be tried without jury and suspects jailed indefinitely without trial. The implications are catastrophic. I have spent many anguished days and sleepless nights wondering what steps we should take that would, non-violently, indicate to the government our determination not to be taken for granted.

Mohan goes on miming an anguished speech; meanwhile, the Mahatma appears and looks at him compassionately.

MAHATMA: (*Softly*) Go on. Tell them how troubled you are. If they derive their strength from you, you derive your strength from them.
MOHAN: (*To audience*) ... deeply troubled. (*Continues miming a speech*)

MAHATMA: You searched everywhere for a way. You searched within.

MOHAN: ... Searched within.

MAHATMA: Then suddenly, in a flash, you realized what must be done.

MOHAN: Then suddenly, in a flash, I realized what must be done. I was sick with worry, lying in bed. In a moment between waking and sleeping an inner voice said to me:

The Mahatma speaks and Mohan mimes the same words simultaneously. The two are now speaking as one, in one voice.

MAHATMA: On a chosen day, let the whole nation come to a standstill—to demonstrate that the will of the people is greater than the might of the government.

The Mahatma disappears.

MOHAN: (*Continuing. To audience*) Let us mark the start of our nationwide satyagraha in absolute peace and quiet and prayer.

Shouts of "Mahatma Gandhi ki jai!" The lights fade.

SCENE 4

A prayer meeting in progress. Mohan is seated facing the audience. A group of men and women can be heard singing the Ram Dhun ("Raghupati raghava raja raam etc.") The singing comes to an end.

MOHAN: The people of India deserve congratulations for the nationwide success of the satyagraha. Everywhere shutters were downed, the streets deserted. In some cities, people gathered in large numbers for peaceful demonstrations—

An agitated Sarojini Naidu enters, waving an open telegram.

SAROJINI: Bapu, Bapu! Terrible news from Punjab! Terrible news.

She hands him the telegram. He reads it with mounting dismay. Then speaks to the audience.

MOHAN: In Amritsar, Sir Michael O'Dyer, governor of the Punjab, allowed the police to fire on a peaceful procession. The crowd went berserk. Carrying its dead, it went on the rampage. It attacked two banks and the railway station. It killed five Europeans and beat up a lady named Miss Sherwood.

SAROJINI: (*Involuntarily*) That O'Dwyer is a stupid man! What else could he expect? If you shoot at the innocent, they are bound to retaliate! It shows the people's resolve. Now the whole nation will rise up in anger—

MOHAN: No, no, no! You are wrong to be pleased. It's a shame! May God show us the way to atone for the sins of our countrymen and may God help us to persuade those who oppose us to see our point of view. Each one of these deaths diminishes us. Revenge is bad. "An eye for an eye" will only leave the whole world blind.

SAROJINI: But, Gandhiji, the police fired on the crowd.

MOHAN: That is no excuse. We must first curb our own urge to violence and turn it into love, real love, for the opponent. You are a poet. The English poet Shelley has advice that would hold good for any satyagrahi. He says:

> "With folded arms and steady eyes,
> And little fear, and less surprise,
> Look upon them as they slay
> Till their rage has died away.
>
> "Then they will return with shame
> To the place from which they came,
> And the blood thus shed will speak
> In hot blushes on their cheek."

The lights fade.

SCENE 5

To one side of the stage, a spot comes on. An anguished Jawaharlal Nehru, dressed in khadi kurta and dhoti, is on an old-style telephone. He has obviously been reading the newspaper.

JAWAHAR: But, Sarojini, Bapu cannot hold back now. Have you read today's paper? O'Dwyer has capped the whole thing with another atrocity. A massacre! He got General Dyer and his troops to fire without warning into a peaceful crowd of twenty thousand men, women and children in an enclosed public park. The crowd was trapped with no exit available to it. The troops....

In the centre of the stage a larger spot comes on to show a man and a woman standing with their backs to the audience. In the woman's arms is a life-like doll swaddled in clothes and presumed to be her baby.

On the sound system we hear the rapid tread of military boots as soldiers take up positions "on the double".

Two silhouettes of soldiers of the Gurkha regiment enter the central spot and kneel with their backs to the audience. They are facing the backs of the man and woman, who turn slowly in surprise as the soldiers raise their rifles.

On the sound system, we hear the continuous firing begin, mixed with the screams, wails and cries of the injured and dying.

The persons are killed or wounded repeatedly in a variety of ways till it becomes a macabre dance of death to the rhythm of the gunfire. We hear the voice of General Dyer saying, "Well done, well done! Keep going. Take good aim. Reload. Fire at will. Don't let them get away."

JAWAHAR: ...continued firing for ten minutes till their ammunition was exhausted.

The sound system relays the abating gunfire that ends with one or two concluding isolated shots. The sounds of the weeping and wailing of the shocked and injured and grief-stricken. And the wail of a child, taken up at a distance by the crying of another.

The soldiers leave. The bodies lie inert.

JAWAHAR: The ground was littered with thousands of bodies. Of these, according to official estimates, more than one thousand two hundred were seriously injured and three hundred and ninety-seven were dead. Strict curfew has been enforced over the city. No one is allowed to go to the aid of the injured or carry away the dead.

The spot fades.

SCENE 6

Sarojini and Mohan.

MOHAN: If Plassey laid the foundation of the British Empire, Amritsar has shaken it.

SAROJINI: Rioting has broken out in various parts of the country. Just give the clarion call and the whole nation will rise—

MOHAN: No, no, we must control ourselves. Not for me a freedom won on the wings of violence. And what freedom is that? For what we seek is freedom *from* violence. I have made a Himalayan blunder in thinking the people could practice civil disobedience without proper guidance in non-violence. I am suspending satyagraha immediately and undertaking a fast for three days as penance for my mistake. Go and inform the others that the movement is suspended indefinitely till we have learnt to improve ourselves.

She goes. Jawahar rushes in.

JAWAHAR: My first thought on being released from prison was to come to you, Gandhiji. We've got to talk. We've got to understand each other. Sometimes you leave me completely bewildered.

MOHAN: Ah, Jawaharlal. Come, sit by me. What bewilders you?

JAWAHAR: (*Sitting down quickly*) The way you think and speak. Now take the deeds of this government.

MOHAN: This government is satanic.

JAWAHAR: There you are—satanic! What a word to use! You bring religious, indeed biblical, terminology into a description or denunciation of a horrendous aspect of our political reality.

MOHAN: Do I embarrass you by using one simple word instead of twenty intellectually-acceptable ones?

JAWAHAR: Well, yes. The fact of the matter is you use emotionally loaded words from the vocabulary of ethics.

MOHAN: Shouldn't ethics enter politics and indeed govern it?

JAWAHAR: But where I would say an act was wrong or bad, you would carry it into another dimension by calling it evil.

MOHAN: Was the massacre at Jallianwallah Bagh not evil?

JAWAHAR: You see what I mean? We have to confront a social reality in a socially realistic way. But you carry it into the epic dimension by turning it into a struggle between good and evil.

MOHAN: Are we not engaged in an epic struggle?

JAWAHAR: Every day?

MOHAN: Every day. Even in our lives.

JAWAHAR: I have great difficulty explaining your methods. They seem more like morals than means for achieving a goal. Now just take your insistence on non-violence.

People are impatient. They have been saying for a long time that we should take up arms against the British—

MOHAN: And I have been saying for an equally long time that they are wrong. That approach will only result in worsening our bondage. Guns and bombs spread terror, and terrorists are answered with more terror. It is a vicious cycle that only creates fundamentalists and fanatics.

JAWAHAR: But these are not right wing people I am talking about. They say look at the teachings of Marx, Lenin. See what happened in Soviet Russia—an armed revolution. I tell them, if we had the weapons we would use them but, since we don't, we might as well be non-violent.

MOHAN: No, no, no! Even if we had recourse to weapons, we must be non-violent. A fully-armed man is very likely to be at heart a coward. Possession of arms implies an element of fear, if not cowardice. But non-violence is unadulterated fearlessness.

JAWAHAR: But to fight the British, don't we need—?

MOHAN: We are not fighting the British. It is not the British people who are ruling India; it is modern civilization with its exploitative system of railways, telegraphs, telephones and almost every invention which has been claimed to be a triumph. The people of Europe, before they were touched by this so-called modern civilization, had much in common with the people of the East. Even now Europeans like

Kallenbach who break through the materialism of modern civilization and are not touched by its crassness are far better able to mix with Indians. Today, unfortunately, there is no such thing left as Western or European civilization; it is only modern civilization which is purely material. Among the British there are many men and women who value and practice the true Christian ethic. These are our friends and comrades in the struggle. People such as C. F. Andrews, West, Polak and many thousands like them. Whether British or Indian, we are together in this fight against the system. Behind the guns of imperialism and colonialism is the system.

JAWAHAR: The Marxists call it capitalism.

MOHAN: Marxism is itself materialistic and therefore part of the trap. The real freedom struggle is to be free of materialism.

JAWAHAR: Frankly, Bapu, your views seem to me to be completely unreal.

MOHAN: (*Smiles*) Then why do you follow me?

JAWAHAR: Because your idealism moves me and I see it means no harm to anyone and I haven't the heart to disillusion you. And there seems to be nothing better on the horizon.

MOHAN: (*Laughs*) At least you're truthful. That's the first qualification for a satyagrahi.

JAWAHAR: And what is the second?

MOHAN: Non-violence. I'm told you have a terrible temper.

JAWAHAR: Oh, just tantrums. I tend to be impatient. Can't abide fools.

MOHAN: Well, you'll have to put up with me.

They laugh. The lights fade.

SCENE 7

A string bed. Beside it, hidden under a sheet, a large object that could be a piece of furniture or some contraption. On the floor near the bed is a basin of water and a small folded towel. On a low table is a thali of peeled oranges that have been deseeded.

Kasturba enters and stands aside to let Mohan in. He walks with little indications of pain.

KASTURBA: Go on in. Sit down. I have a surprise for you. (*Turns to some others in the wings*) Everybody else, please stay out. He needs rest. (*To Mohan*) Go, go. Sit. I'll wash your feet and massage them with oil. You look tired. Why're you limping?

MOHAN: Well, well, you've become quite bossy. I'm sure they call you the dictator of Sabarmati Ashram.

KASTURBA: Oh my God! What are all those cuts and scratches on your feet?

MOHAN: You won't believe it.

KASTURBA: Tell me.

MOHAN: (*Sits down*) Politicians in England and America

often get sore hands from having to greet whole crowds of well-wishers. Fortunately, here we just do namaste. But when you're called a Mahatma, everybody falls at your feet.

Kasturba bursts out laughing and brings a hand to her mouth in surprise.

KASTURBA: You mean, they claw and scratch your feet?
MOHAN: Feet, legs, arms. Going through a crowd is like walking a path of thorns and brambles.
KASTURBA: Poor you! But they mean well. They love you. (*Pulls the basin into position*) Here, let me wash your feet. And, instead of oil, let me rub some medicine into the wounds.
MOHAN: You said you had a surprise for me.
KASTURBA: Go on, lift the cover. It's a present sent to you by a friend.

He goes and lifts the cover and stands back puzzled. He looks at the contraption.

MOHAN: What is it?
KASTURBA: Even I thought at first that it was some kind of wooden bicycle. But it is what you have been looking for all these years. At last Gangabehn Majumdar found it in someone's loft.

MOHAN: The spinning wheel! This is the ancient time-honoured spinning wheel! The peasant woman's friend. The farmer's secondary occupation. The poor man's source of income.

KASTURBA: I knew you would be pleased.

MOHAN: Pleased? I'm overjoyed. When my inner voice first told me to look for it more than ten years ago, I wrote about it and called it a handloom—not knowing the difference. So this is a spinning wheel! (*Tries it*) How does it work?

KASTURBA: No one knows. Everyone at the ashram has tried it.

MOHAN: Surely one of the weavers at the ashram has some idea how—

KASTURBA: They all know how to weave cloth on a loom. They know about bobbins and shuttles. But they don't know how to spin yarn on a wheel. We still buy all our yarn from the mills. It comes in slivers.

MOHAN: Oh what a tragedy! Here I am, hoping to recover a lost art for which India was famous. An art that was deliberately destroyed by the colonialists. Folklore says they cut off the thumbs of our weavers in order to create a market for the mass produced goods of Western industrialization. Here I am, trying to find a way for India's millions to, once again, be self-reliant, self-sufficient—and we still have to depend on mills for the thread with which we could make our own cloth! In the secret of the ancient spinning wheel is the salvation of India.

KASTURBA: You know what I am thinking? (*He looks at her, waiting*) You have at last learnt how to make good speeches!

MOHAN: (*Laughs*) And you know the secret of that? (*She waits*) You. You have given me something to say *(He indicates the spinning wheel).*

The lights fade.

SCENE 8

Jawahar and Sarojini and a couple of spinning wheels. In the background are people spinning.

JAWAHAR: The chakra—the spinning wheel! I don't understand. Is this some kind of mystical symbolism? I don't believe in mysticism and even less in prophets. What does he mean—India can be rid of the British government within a year if the whole country takes to non-cooperation but it can only be free economically if it takes to the spinning wheel? Sometimes I wonder if the whole country isn't going crazy, following this man who comes up with peculiar new concepts –

SAROJINI: And new words.

JAWAHAR: Exactly! He has to coin new words because the political actions are new.

SAROJINI: First, it was passive resistance in South Africa that became satyagraha. Then we had an All-India *hartal* (*strike*) and now non-cooperation.

JAWAHAR: Absurd! And fascinating. I mean, co-operation is already a hyphenated word. Then we put a non in front of it and another hyphen. A word with two hyphens!

SAROJINI: Well, if the Soviets, after their revolution, are busy setting up cooperatives, we can set up non-cooperatives!

Both of them go into peals of laughter. The lights fade.

SCENE 9

Jawaharlal Nehru and Mohammed Ali Jinnah in discussion over tea and sandwiches. Between them is a silver tea set. Jinnah is thin, tall and dressed dapperly in a light summer suit. Nehru is in churidar pyjamas and kurta with jacket and cap.

JAWAHAR: Stop surveying me with that knowing sneer, Jinnah. I should've realized all this would be beyond you.

JINNAH: Not at all, dear fellow. I know what you're about, along with that sanctimonious mentor of yours. You're trying to be like him and grab the heart of the masses.

JAWAHAR: I do wish you wouldn't speak of him like that. He's the most honest person I've ever met.

JINNAH: Anyway, do you really mean the days of Saville Row suits are over? (*A small dry laugh*) Whenever you come into the bar library, some joker or other remarks with awe that your clothes are tailored in London, laundered in Paris and made useless in India.

JAWAHAR: (*Laughs*) You know perfectly well, Jinnah, that that stuff about laundering in Paris is an absolute canard. They used to say it about my father, and now they say it of me.

JINNAH: But *you've* gone completely to the bolsheviks, or should I say the monks? How on earth do you stand that rough cloth next to your skin?

JAWAHAR: Home spun, handmade khadi. I'm proud of it. Looking forward to the day I can spin yards of it myself.

JINNAH: And I daresay you'll wear that silly cap on your head for the rest of your life. The prison insignia rather than the school tie.

JAWAHAR: Gandhi has made prison the most exclusive school in the world.

JINNAH: Bravo! Well said! But really I do think many of Gandhi's actions are wrong. For instance, he's trying too hard to become a spokesman for the muslims of India. He is leading India to calamity.

JAWAHAR: That's a bit far-fetched. What on earth do you mean?

JINNAH: Let's look at it coldly, dispassionately, like the lawyers we are.

Jawahar picks up a sandwich and walks about nibbling at it.

JAWAHAR: Go ahead. Surprise me, stun me. Make out your case.

JINNAH: Turkey sided with Germany in the war and was defeated.

JAWAHAR: No denying that. Rotten mistake on the part of Turkey. Bad decision by the Caliph.

JINNAH: Since the Caliph of Turkey is considered the head of Islam, a couple of muslims in India, the two Ali brothers, started a movement in support of the Caliphate, demanding that the British accord it better terms and treatment. This movement, as you know, has come to be called the Khilafat. Now, Gandhi, in order to get a hold of the emotions of the Muslims has taken up the Khilafat movement as his own. Nowhere in the rest of the world is such a fuss being made as here. Gandhi is helping to internationalize Indian Muslims. This is a religious movement. Sooner or later, the mullahs will step in and extremists will take over. It is a dangerous trend that none of us will be able to control. To play with religion is to play with dynamite.

JAWAHAR: Hm. And how is all this affecting you?

JINNAH: Badly. He ... frightens me. I have never been staunch or religious. But the more of a Mahatma he becomes, the more of a Muslim I must be.

The lights fade.

SCENE 10

An ante-chamber in the Viceregal Palace. John Clancy, in full uniform, stands before a large blackboard on which various names have been written in clear capital letters with chalk. The names are: GANDHI, MOTILAL NEHRU, JINNAH, SAPRU, JAWAHARLAL NEHRU, PATEL, SUBHAS BOSE, SRINIVASA IYENGAR, FAZLI HUSAIN, AMBEDKAR. *Clancy nervously tidies one or two letters with the aid of duster and chalk. Then steps back to study his handiwork. Lord Irwin, the viceroy, enters.*

VICEROY: Ah, there you are, Clancy.

CLANCY: (*Spins round, dropping duster and chalk*) Good heavens! Lord Irwin. (*Collects his wits, salutes*) Your Excellency. Sorry about that. (*Picks up duster and chalk*) You gave me a bit of a start.

VICEROY: A bit of a start? Why? Don't you expect to see the viceroy in the Viceregal Palace?

CLANCY: Of course, milord. But I was told you were busy with the members of the Simon Commission. So I didn't expect you for another hour at least.

VICEROY: (*With a look to heaven*) Don't remind me. (*Sighs and sits down*) I've got half of Westminster in there it seems—Sir John Simon, Major Atlee, Burnham, etcetera, etcetera. It's not easy answering the questions of a whole gaggle of MPs. They're having a break for tea now so I stepped out. We need to see if we can give them something pleasant to think about.

CLANCY: (*Carefully*) Are they ... very distressed, milord, with all the black flag demonstrations that are greeting them?

VICEROY: Distressed? Clancy, they are devastated. In Lucknow, when we banned demonstrations in the street, the protesters flew black kites. They dropped the kites at the governor's garden party. On the kites was written: 'Simon go back!' Old Gandhi's really got guts, swinging the cat by its tail under their very noses.

The viceroy wipes his forehead with a handkerchief, blows his nose then stares at Clancy.

CLANCY: (*Uncomfortable*) Something the matter, Your Excellency?

VICEROY: Good God, Clancy, I just realised it! You're in full dress uniform, medals and ribbons and all. Why? (*Squints to focus on a name-plate*) You've even got a breast-plate with name and designation. (*Reads*) John Clancy, Chief of Intelligence, C.I.D., comma H.M.P.S.—

CLANCY: Criminal Investigation Department, His Majesty's Police Service.

VICEROY: (*Patiently*) I know that, Clancy. I know that. But why are you today advertizing your normally secretive self and secret activities with such careless abandon?

CLANCY: You said something about providing guidance to the Honourable Members of Parliament—

VICEROY: Ah! I see. You were hoping to be called in in your advisory capacity. Well, old boy, I'm afraid I must keep you to myself and pass your advice on as coming from me. Discretion, dear fellow, is always the better part. And ... er ... as for your promotion, leave it to me. It'll happen.

CLANCY: (*Controlling a twitch in his face*) Thank you, Your Excellency.

VICEROY: Now then, let's get on with the job. What hope can we offer Sir John Simon?

CLANCY: Frankly, Lord Irwin, the Simon Commission is a dud. It's here to interview Indians to see if they are fit for self-government and to devise a plan that, while preserving the Raj, accommodates Indian aspirations.

VICEROY: Quite.

CLANCY: But the Indians have boycotted the Commission. Because, among all the members, there's not one Indian.

VICEROY: Can't have that, old boy. These are all members of the British parliament.

CLANCY: It could have included Lord Sinha. He's an Indian. And an M.P. Furthermore, members can always be co-opted. So the Commission is an eye-wash. No wonder, the Indian politicians are united against the Simon Commission.

VICEROY: So, what's the answer?

CLANCY: Create disunity among the politicians.

VICEROY: (*Laughs*) A wonderful thought! But how?

Clancy moves to the blackboard.

CLANCY: These are the Indian politicians who are leading various movements. One look at the board will give Sir John Simon and the others a quick overview of the main currents at work in India.
VICEROY: Come to the nitty-gritty, Clancy. How can the Raj hold out and succeed against this motley crew?
CLANCY: (*Glancing at the board*) The only one with real mass backing is Gandhi. The others are all debating society boys.
VICEROY: How do we defuse Gandhi?
CLANCY: I've got some dirt on him. I've got some dirt on everyone.
VICEROY: Gandhi makes diamonds of his dirt. You can't blackmail him. He writes it all out himself in his paper *Young India*. You can't pressure him except through his conscience. The only time I've known him to back off is when he is shocked by the violence of his own followers. Would you agree with that, Clancy?
CLANCY: That's right, milord. Chauri Chaura. The mob went wild, attacked a police station, killed twenty-one Indian policemen. Gandhi stopped the whole movement and went on a fast. He didn't want his followers injuring or taking the life of anyone, not even a policeman who may have fired at them. Now, sir, I'm a policeman and that thought touches me deeply.

VICEROY: Be careful, Clancy. That's the thin edge of the wedge. The man gets a hold of your heart.

CLANCY: I must tell you, milord, that sometimes my men have been in a terrible jam, what with the crowds being protective of their Mahatma. And it's Gandhi who saves them. He says, "Release the poor fellow. He's only a plainclothes policeman snooping on me. He's a detective from the C.I.D. Let him do his job. I have nothing to hide."

VICEROY: What is the dirt you have on him?

CLANCY: It's his son really. The eldest one. Harilal. He goes to prostitutes. He drinks. He brawls.

VICEROY: Hm. But still that's not a crime. (*Wrily*) It's quite common in old blighty.

CLANCY: He's broken away from his father. Gandhi has practically disowned him. He's written to him publicly to mend his ways.

VICEROY: I see. What else?

CLANCY: Harilal has defrauded some persons who trusted him. He set up a company in Calcutta then went off with the money his partners had put in.

VICEROY: Does Gandhi know?

CLANCY: Oh yes. The victims naturally complained to him. But he published their complaint in his newspaper and warned people against the folly of thinking a son must be like the father. He said he took no responsibility for his son. The son has now become a Muslim.

VICEROY: What? Good heavens, that must've given old Gandhi a turn. But he can hardly do anything about it. (*Wrily*) Well, he'd better begin with Hindu-Muslim unity in his own house.

CLANCY: He's doing that, Your Excellency. If Harilal is a Muslim, Gandhi wants him to be a good Muslim.

VICEROY: I'm afraid that's not much good to us. And Motilal Nehru? Anything on him?

CLANCY:: He's been seen eating beef.

VICEROY: Come, come, Clancy. You're talking about something I do practically everyday.

CLANCY: But it's different for him, Your Excellency. He's a Hindu. He could lose every election within the Congress and outside it. In fact, when Gandhi made the Congress support the Muslims in their Khilafat movement, there was talk of getting the Muslims to return the favour by giving up the killing of cows.

VICEROY: I didn't know that. Has that come about?

CLANCY: No. Gandhi put a stop to all that. He said he was supporting the Muslims because he believed in their cause not because he wanted to barter his support.

VICEROY: Come on, Clancy, I've got to get back in there and face the blithering M.Ps. Have you a strategy to suggest?

CLANCY: (*Indicating the names on the board*) I suggest we pit them all against each other.

VICEROY: Of course, my dear chap. *Divis et impera*. But they've just had an all-party convention in order to forge unity and national identity. They've adopted the Report of the Motilal Nehru Committee as a blue print for India's constitution. It says all adults will have the right to vote. And, mind you, that includes women. We don't have it in Britain and they're demanding it here!

Clancy has been thinking. He goes to the blackboard, takes a stick of chalk and circles two names—Fazli Husain and Ambedkar.

CLANCY: Tell Sir John Simon to back these two and you'll be able to control the rest. (*Politely*) Of course, I'm only suggesting what Your Excellency already has in mind.

VICEROY: Of course. And what have I in mind?

CLANCY: You wish to hunt Jinnah through Fazli and Gandhi through Ambedkar.

VICEROY: And will that bring them down?

CLANCY: No. But it might tame down to your will. Then the divided Muslims and the divided Hindus can be played off against each other.

VICEROY: (*Thinks*) Hm. (*A look of pleasure*) Thank you, Clancy, this blackboard was a brilliant idea of yours. Clarifies everything. Come, let me walk you to the door. (*Puts an arm round Clancy's shoulders and begins walking out with him*) Now, dear Clancy, if I suggested to Sir John Simon that Fazli Husain, who represents the socially and economically backward strata of

Muslims living mainly in the rural areas, should have electoral safeguards that guaranteed…

The lights fade out.

SCENE 11

The Mahatma and Mohan. Mohan worried. The Mahatma harrying him.

MAHATMA: They are trying to divide the opposition. They won't listen to you. You are beating your head against a wall. Lord Irwin, the Viceroy, has rejected the demands for a constitution and dominion status. It's all a trick to keep you talking endlessly. You are no nearer self-government than when you returned from South Africa. You're older by fifteen years. You surprise yourself in the mirror when you see an ageing man. You are sixty-one … already!

MOHAN: I must act decisively.

MAHATMA: Yes, act. Not talk.

MOHAN: But what action?

MAHATMA: Something simple, direct, forceful, that unites the country behind you. Now that Congress has resolved to seek complete independence, go for that.

MOHAN: Jawaharlal has forced the pace. I would still settle for dominion status if only the British would—

MAHATMA: At a sign from you let the whole country erupt with Civil Disobedience—a festival of self-assertion!

MOHAN: We have tried selling banned literature.

MAHATMA: Too intellectual. The peasants must take part. The illiterate masses must wake.

MOHAN: We have considered breaking the revenue laws and the—

MAHATMA: No, no, no. That's all very well for the propertied and wealthy but what about the oppressed, those who have nothing but bread and salt and water? Let them join you in a massive upheaval.

MOHAN: We need to find a law to break. There is no law against baking your own bread. Every farmer who grows any grain can grind it and make his own roti. And water is free.

MAHATMA: But salt is not. Though it is found in nature and can be harvested from the sea, salt is taxed. You have to buy it from a licensed government source. So a poor man pays a tax on what he could just make himself.

MOHAN: What shall I do?

MAHATMA: Break the salt law. Momentously. And let the country join in.

MOHAN: Hm. (*A slight pause*) Hm. (*Then more positively*) Hm!

MAHATMA: Of course, you must first give the viceroy a chance to repeal the Salt Laws. It's only fair. Write him a letter.

MOHAN: (*Nods*) Hm.

SCENE 12

Jawaharlal Nehru seated crosslegged beside a spinning wheel and a book which he seems to have pushed aside only a few moments ago. He is peering at another book lying open near him. At the same time he is pouring water from a bottle into a jug. Over the mouth of the jug is a cloth with which he seems to be straining the water.

Sarojini enters carrying a pile of newspapers.

SAROJINI: Jambo, as my African friends would say! Greetings to you, dear Jawahar!

JAWAHAR: Ssh ssh ssh. (*Concentrates on pouring the water*) So you're back from your travels in Africa. I hear your mission was a great success.

SAROJINI: Thanks to the renown of the Little Wizard. That's how they think of him—the little wiz who defeated the demon of racial discrimination. People of all colours—black, brown, yellow, white—welcomed me with open arms. Most touching. (*A pause*) What are you doing? Don't you know the Great March has begun? The papers are full of it. I thought we'd read about it together and discuss what we have to do next. (*Throws the papers down*)

JAWAHAR: (*Carefully, while preoccupied*) I am doing what I have to do next.

SAROJINI: You mean...?

JAWAHAR: Exactly. (*Puts the bottle down*) I've finally found a book that explains how you manufacture salt. (Sarojini laughs) Either you just find it and mine it. Or you take some salty water and...

Sarojini goes into peals of laughter.

SAROJINI: That's hilarious!

JAWAHAR: It's not. I'd just managed to learn how to spin. Look, there's my quota of yarn for the day. I might even weave a saree for my wife Kamala. And now I find that in order to be free, I must also make salt.

SAROJINI: (*Laughs*) We're all caught in the web of love spun by the mystic spinner. I'm impressed. (*Sits down and begins glancing through the various newspapers. Meanwhile*) But most of all, Jawahar, I'm impressed at how much he has changed you. I first heard of you in England as Joe. Someone said to me, you must meet young Joe Nehru, a terrific chap –

JAWAHAR: Ah, that must've been about the time someone said to me, you must read Sarah Naidu's poetry, she writes divinely. (*Shrugs*) I had read Sarojini but never heard of Sarah. And I was damned if I was going to read Sarah Naidu's poetry!

SAROJINI: (*Laughs*) So we admit it was Sammy who gave us the confidence to be ourselves, our beautiful selves.

JAWAHAR: (*Warningly*) Easy, easy. Don't get narcissistic. We're still finding ourselves. But I thought we were talking of Bapu. Who's Sammy?

SAROJINI: As they say, "One and the same." Our mystic master, the mickey mouse Mahatma.

JAWAHAR: I wish you wouldn't talk of him like that.

SAROJINI: Oh? And you're the one against all titles and awards and hero worship. Now you're telling me not to speak lightly of *the Mahatma*!

JAWAHAR: I didn't mean that, at all. I just meant all that alliteration jars on me. "Mystic master, mickey mouse Mahatma" (*Irritably*) I'm told you sometimes address him as the spiritual spinning spider and sign yourself as the woeful wistful wanderer.

SAROJINI: (*Sulking*) I'm not really offended. Just pretending.

JAWAHAR: (*Laughs*) Anyway, isn't it amazing? Bapu decides on a pinch of salt to shake an empire but he adds the drama of a 240-mile walk to it.

SAROJINI: 240 miles at 10 miles a day means 24 days. By then the world will be waiting for that pinch of salt.

JAWAHAR: *Magnifique!* The walk of Napoleon from Elba.

SAROJINI: Moses leading the Israelites out of bondage.

JAWAHAR: Where does he get this instinct for theatre?

SAROJINI: Well, his leadership certainly brings about a "willing suspension of disbelief". I think he's the greatest wonder of the world. I couldn't think otherwise. And I'm going to join him at Dandi for that historic moment.

The lights fade.

SCENE 13

The viceroy is studying some documents. John Clancy enters.

CLANCY: Milord.
VICEROY: What is it?
CLANCY: The salt picked up by Gandhi from the beach was auctioned to the highest bidder for one thousand six hundred rupees. People are now not only making salt but buying and selling it.
VICEROY: What? Arrest the sellers, arrest the buyers.
CLANCY: People all over the country are making salt in pots and pans. They are encouraged by leaflets giving directions, prepared by Jawaharlal Nehru. He's president of the Congress.
VICEROY: Arrest him.
CLANCY: Right now in Bombay there's a crowd of about sixty thousand gathering on the beach.
VICEROY: Arrest them.
CLANCY: We won't have enough handcuffs, sir.
VICEROY: Use rope.
CLANCY: In Ahmedabad, ten thousand persons have bought salt from the Congress office.
VICEROY: Dealing in salt is illegal. So is its manufacture. Arrest them all. (*Slapping the documents*) Indian corporators are resigning from the Legislative Assembly. Indian officials are quitting the civil service.

I can't be worrying about every petty offender who is selling salt.

CLANCY: Exactly, sir. That's why I wondered whether we should let this dispatch from Webb Miller go through.

VICEROY: Who?

CLANCY: He's American.

VICEROY: What the dickens are the Americans doing here?

CLANCY: He's a foreign correspondent for the United Press.

VICEROY: Ah.

CLANCY: The dispatch is an eye-witness account. He actually made his way to the salt pans at Dharasana. After Dandi, they announced they would do the same at Dharasana.

VICEROY: I thought we arrested Gandhi to prevent that?

CLANCY: Sir, we did. But the person now in command is the poetess Sarojini Naidu.

A bearer brings in a silver tray.

VICEROY: Ah, breakfast. Care to join me?

CLANCY: I've eaten, sir.

VICEROY: Coffee?

CLANCY: (*Considers*) Er ... no, thank you.

VICEROY: Well, that's one of the problems of being a viceroy. Finding the time to eat between all the crises affecting an administration.

CLANCY: I'm sorry to have called so early, sir

VICEROY: Not at all. I'd rather be informed than taken by surprise.

He waves the bearer away. The man leaves.

CLANCY: Shall I leave it on your table, sir?
VICEROY: What? The dispatch? No, no, read it to me while I eat. (*Laughs*) Can't delay a decision when Americans are involved. They have no patience.

Clancy smiles, takes out his spectacles, puts them on and begins reading aloud. The viceroy eats and has his coffee, reacting in various ways to what he hears. He is pained and upset, and eventually cannot continue with his breakfast.

CLANCY: This is what he says. (*Reads*)

> *"Four hundred native police commanded by half a dozen British officials stood ready by the salt pans.*
>
> *Suddenly, at a word of command, scores of native police rushed upon the advancing marchers and rained blows on their heads with their steel-shod lathis. Not one of the marchers even raised an arm to fend off the blows. They went down like tenpins. From where I stood I heard the sickening whacks of the clubs on unprotected skulls. The waiting crowd of watchers*

groaned and sucked in their breaths in sympathetic pain at every blow.

Those struck down fell sprawling, unconscious or writhing in pain with fractured skulls or broken shoulders. In two or three minutes the ground was quilted with bodies. Great patches of blood widened on their white clothes ..."

VICEROY: Enough! My God, Clancy, I can't believe we're doing this! This is what Gandhi meant by "preparing the people for non-violence". It makes me sick to my stomach! I've got to find a way to lift the ban on the Congress Working Committee and hold talks with Gandhi.

CLANCY: I thought the idea was to by-pass him, sir.

VICEROY: It was, dear boy. It *was*. Everything changes in politics. Perspectives. Everything.

CLANCY: Complicated game, sir.

VICEROY: I'll get Gandhi out of jail and invite him over for talks.

CLANCY: About the dispatch, sir...?

VICEROY: What? Oh. Painful. Very painful. But let it go. Shows the kind of doggedness we are dealing with. (*Thinks, then*) Damn it! Absolutely ruined my breakfast!

The lights fade.

SCENE 14

Mohan and the viceroy seated comfortably across from each other. The viceroy is sipping a cup of tea. Mohan has a glass of lemon juice.

VICEROY: Well, I'm so glad we could agree at last. Nearly ten thosand prisoners will be released, you'll call off your civil disobedience and the Congress will participate in the next Round Table Conference in London. This is just what I had been praying for. You know, Mr. Gandhi, I pray every night, just as my mother taught me, kneeling by my bed.

MOHAN: It's always a joy when prayers are answered.

VICEROY: One of the journalists called this "a meeting of two saints".

MOHAN: (*Smiles*) That is news, indeed. At least to me.

VICEROY: (*Laughs*) Of course, when you go to England to attend the Round Table Conference it may be a good idea for you to accept an invitation from His Majesty the King-Emperor, should he wish to see you. Shall I say that you will?

MOHAN: When I am in another man's country I can hardly refuse to be polite to him. He is my host.

VICEROY: Good. That's settled then. Mr. Gandhi, allow me to toast your health in the finest Indian tea. (*Raises his cup*)

MOHAN: Thank you. (*The viceroy drinks*) And allow me to

toast your health in this excellent lime-juice flavoured with a pinch of salt … (*He takes a little salt from a pouch*) … of my own illegal manufacture. This reminds me of the Boston Tea Party.

He drops the salt in the nimbu-pani, smiles and raises the glass and drinks. The viceroy's smile remains frozen.

SCENE 15

A group of journalists and photographers, most of them British, are looking anxiously for Gandhi to emerge from some direction or other. 'There he is!' says one and the group rushes that way. 'Over here' and the rush is reversed. 'That's him, I think' has some moving to check. One calls out 'Mr. Gandhi' and all turn to look. Mohan enters and strides across the stage. He is soon surrounded by the press. He stops good-naturedly.

JOURNALIST 1: Do you have any message you'd like to give?

MOHAN: My life is my message.

JOURNALIST 1: Mr. Gandhi, didn't you feel a little underdressed for your interview with the king?

MOHAN: The king had enough on for both of us.

JOURNALIST 2: Mr. Gandhi, the Round Table Conference seems to be a failure. It has not been able to agree a Constitution for India. Are you sorry you came to England?

MOHAN: No. My real conference is with the people of Britain and I am happy to talk to them on the streets as I am pleased to talk to you.

JOURNALIST 1: General Smuts of South Africa met you here in London a few days ago. What did he say to you?

MOHAN: (*Smiles*) He said, "I did not give you such a bad time as you gave me."

JOURNALIST 3: Must you wear that loin-cloth? Couldn't you get yourself a pair of trousers?

MOHAN: You people wear plus-fours, mine are minus-fours.

They laugh.

JOURNALIST 2: We hear you used to walk a good five miles to the Viceregal Palace in Delhi for your meetings with the viceroy. Here too, you walk every morning through the East End and the children follow you dancing—

MOHAN: It makes me feel like the Pied Piper.

JOURNALIST 2: —what do they say to you?

MOHAN: Uncle Gandhi, what do you eat?

JOURNALIST 2: And what do you answer?

MOHAN: Dates and dried fruit with goat's milk. They also ask if I will come to their birthday parties.

JOURNALIST 2: Is it true that they sent you presents on your birthday?

MOHAN: They did. And they came and sang songs and lit candles. (*Chuckles*) They find me amusing.

JOURNALIST 3: Bernard Shaw the playwright says he was shocked speechless to discover that you were, in his words, "not a man but a phenomenon." What did he discuss with you?

MOHAN: Many topics. All with great wit and humor.

JOURNALIST 1: In Lancashire, to everyone's surprise, you sparked among the people a great warmth of affection.

MOHAN: I shall treasure the memory of their love to the end of my earthly existence.

JOURNALIST 1: What did you say to them?

MOHAN: I said to them let me tell you the truth like a true friend. You have three million unemployed, but we have nearly 300 million unemployed. How am I to talk of God to the millions who have to go without two meals a day? To them God can only appear as bread and butter. Well, the peasants of India were getting their bread from their soil. I offered them the spinning wheel in order that they may get the butter, and if I appear today before the British public in my loin-cloth, it is because I have come as the sole representative of those half-starved, half-naked, dumb millions.

The journalists burst into spontaneous applause. The lights fade.

SCENE 16

The Viceroy Lord Irwin in Delhi. Clancy enters.

CLANCY: Gandhi is back in India, sir. He says he's returned empty-handed because he was sent shopping with an unsigned cheque. He says you got him to go to the Round Table Conference on a false hope, an undefined promise.

VICEROY: What's he going to do about it?

CLANCY: Resume civil disobedience.

VICEROY: He turns it on and off like a tap, doesn't he? Arrest them all. Immediately. Gandhi. His wife. Nehru. Sarojini Naidu. The lot.

CLANCY: Yes, sir.

VICEROY: And tell Gandhi bluntly that we don't consider him a representative of all Indians. He does not represent the Muslims. Nor does he represent the outcastes, the untouchables.

CLANCY: Right, sir.

VICEROY: He'll have plenty of time to read in jail so whack him with this. (*Handing Clancy a document*) It's a copy of the new constitution suggested by the prime minister, Ramsay Macdonald. It puts Gandhi in his place. Let me know how he responds. If he has any response.

Lights fade.

SCENE 17

Mohan seated cross-legged by a tree in a jail courtyard, spinning. Before him is a group of three prisoners, facing him, also spinning.

Beside Mohan is the document the viceroy sent.

MOHAN: Now they seek by this document, the so-called draft constitution, to turn India into separate communal electorates and caste divisions. Here, in Yerawada jail, I say to you my brothers, as I have said elsewhere before, I am a bania, and there is no limit to my greed. It had always been my dream and heart's desire to speak not only for 210 million but for the 300 million Indians. Today you may not accept that position of mine. But I may assure you that I have always spoken for Hindu-Muslim unity and for the removal of untouchability. So do not dismiss it merely as a craze of my old age. My heart is confident that God will grant me that position when I may speak for the whole of India, and if I have to die striving for that ideal, I shall achieve the peace of my heart.

The lights fade.

SCENE 18

The viceroy at dinner. Clancy enters.

VICEROY: Is it that urgent, Clancy?
CLANCY: I'm afraid so, sir. It's about Gandhi's response, sir.
VICEROY: Well? (*Laughs*) He's in jail, isn't he? Safely out of harm's way. What can he do?
CLANCY: He's announced a fast unto death, sir.
VICEROY: Unto death? (*Putting down his cutlery*) By jove!
CLANCY: News of it is spreading like wildfire all over the country.
VICEROY: But what can they do about it?
CLANCY: He says he wants caste Hindus to embrace untouchables and do away with untouchability.
VICEROY: Just like that? Overnight? Something that has existed for thousands of years? Something that cannot be erased by legislation, he now wants to wipe out with one fast. It's like getting the Ku Klux Klan to embrace negroes. Huh.

The viceroy gets up and walks a few paces.

CLANCY: He calls this his "tussle with God', sir.
VICEROY: It's crazy. Absurd. I thought he'd try to get the document changed but he's trying, instead, to change society!

CLANCY: Not much we can do about that, sir.

VICEROY: If he dies ... (Sighs) ... there'll be hell to pay.

CLANCY: There could be civil war.

VICEROY: And all due to MacDonald's communal award. Clancy?

CLANCY: Sir?

VICEROY: He's got to be nursed, especially as he gets weaker. Imagine doing this to us from a jail cell! Have him made as comfortable as regulations allow. Transfer that woman—the poetess.

CLANCY: Sarojini Naidu.

VICEROY: Transfer her to the same jail so she can look after him. And also transfer his wife there. Is there anything I've forgotten?

CLANCY: Your dinner, sir.

VICEROY: Don't be funny, Clancy. I meant about Gandhi and his fast. Does he really call it a fast unto death?

CLANCY: I'm afraid so, sir. He hasn't set any time limit to it.

VICEROY: And what does Ambedkar call it?

CLANCY: A political stunt.

Lights fade.

SCENE 19

Night. Mohan in a prison bed set out in a courtyard. Sarojini Naidu is seated by his head. A saree-enshrouded figure, presumed to be Kasturba, massages his feet. The Mahatma appears.

MAHATMA: The tenth day and you are slipping away already. No longer so young. All of India is suffering. Will you save yourself if they sign an understanding—?

The women look at each other as Mohan sits up weakly. Sarojini takes a pad and pen and writes down what Mohan says.

MOHAN: If the Hindu mind is not yet prepared to banish untouchability root and branch it must sacrifice me without the slightest hesitation.
SAROJINI: (*To Kasturba*) I'll go and give this to Col. Doyle the Inspector General of Prisons so it can be announced.

She goes.

MAHATMA: The announcement will cause a great stir among the people. This is the most critical action of your life. Already, temple after temple is throwing open its doors to untouchables.
MOHAN: Harijans.
MAHATMA: Yes, harijans. Children of God as you have chosen to call them. What a sensible idea to place

ballot boxes outside temples so that the ordinary person can vote on the matter. The count in Bombay alone shows nearly 25,000 for and only 445 against. That's wonderful! In Allahabad twelve temples have welcomed harijans. Soon others will follow. You may not make it all happen in a day or a week but you *have* changed an attitude by this fast. No longer will there be social approval of untouchability. When India is free, invite Ambedkar to help draft the constitution.

The lights fade.

SCENE 20

The viceroy—seated and thoughtful. Clancy enters.

VICEROY: Well? It's the thirteenth day of the fast.
CLANCY: They've arrived at a settlement, milord.
VICEROY: (*Sighs*) Ah. Thank heavens! Did Ambedkar negotiate hard?
CLANCY: He demanded "compensation for compromises". A formula has been evolved. The separate electorate has been eliminated.
VICEROY: Amazing.
CLANCY: But Gandhi says he'll break his fast only after the Cabinet in England agrees to the changes he's made in the document.

VICEROY: My God, he's dictating from jail to the prime minister of Britain!
CLANCY: They've cabled the text to England and are now waiting for an answer.

Suddenly temple bells and other bells start ringing out echoed by yet others. Crackers are heard being let off in the streets and there is the sound of celebration.

VICEROY: I think they've received their answer. And I don't really mind that they've received it direct rather than through the viceroy. It shows that the centre of power in India has shifted. (*Sighs*) Well, I'm glad the response to Gandhi's demand is positive.
CLANCY: Me too, sir. It would've been sad to lose the silly old coot to his own stupidity. It would've been a bit like Christ crucifying himself.
VICEROY:(*Stares at him, then*) Clancy, I think you and I should have a little drink.

SCENE 21

The Mahatma holds out a hand to Mohan and helps him rise from bed.

MAHATMA: Events are galloping forward. There are as many pulls as there are personalities in the politics of the time. Try to steer a clear path.

MOHAN: The middle way is difficult. There is the Muslim League and the Hindu Mahasabha, there are the communists and fascists, the socialists and capitalists, the—

MAHATMA: Don't look to any of them for an answer. Look within. See the poorest in the land; there is your gauge. Your every act must benefit the poorest. Wipe every tear from every eye. Put personal concerns out of your mind.

MOHAN: Difficult. Kasturba does not keep good health. I worry for her. Then there is my eldest. Why does he wound me so? And then he turns the knife in the wound.

MAHATMA: You can no longer call him Harilal. He has discarded his name along with his religion. People call him Maulvi Sahib. He preaches in the streets.

MOHAN: All to spite me.

MAHATMA: No. Be fair to him. He may have decided on that path to salvation.

MOHAN: I shall try to believe that. But on that bleak and remote railway station when the crowd was shouting –

MAHATMA: "Mahatma Gandhi ki jai! Mahatma Gandhi ki jai!"

MOHAN: That lone voice shouted ...

MAHATMA: "Kasturba ki jai! Victory to Kasturba!"

MOHAN: I knew it was he, even before I saw him. He was drunk and bedraggled. He came to the window of the railway carriage and ... held out a half-eaten orange to Kasturba. He said ... (Mohan seems unable to continue)

MAHATMA: "Ma, this is a present for you. No, Ma, don't share it with him. Eat it now, in front of me. Show me you love me."

MOHAN: She ate one bit of it and the rest was still in her hand when the train started. Hari knows I love oranges. Oranges and dates are my favourite fruit. I reached out to take one piece from Kasturba but saw that she had closed her fist over it. The juice was flowing between her fingers as freely as the tears were falling from her eyes.

MAHATMA: She was overwrought, emotionally overcome. Forgive her. Forgive him.

MOHAN: I can forgive them all but can I forgive myself?

He turns round and goes back and sits on the bed.

MAHATMA: (*In an urgent whisper*) Get up, get up. Only if you are in control of yourself are you in control of the situation. Merge your sorrows in larger concerns. We are now in the middle of a second world war. This is not the time to indulge yourself.

Mohan gets up resolutely, takes the staff from the Mahatma and moves forward to stand as though addressing an audience. The Mahatma retreats and disappears.

MOHAN: How can we be dragged into a war for the free world when we ourselves are not free? So the Imperial Government must QUIT INDIA.

SCENE 22

Spots come on individually and separately amid growing cries of "Quit India!"

SAROJINI: In answer to Gandhiji's call, thousands—no, millions—of people are offering satyagraha on the streets of India to protest the presence of the British Raj.

JAWAHAR: Students have left their schools and colleges.

JINNAH: This is absurd! I don't agree with this at all! Lawyers have left the law courts. All administration is at a standstill. Thousands are being arrested and jailed. The jails are full.

JAWAHAR: The government is under great pressure. A Garhwali regiment refused to fire on satyagrahis. The Freedom Movement is like a giant wave sweeping the country. And it doesn't matter that all the leaders are in jail.

The spots fade.

SCENE 23

Late evening. Mohan seated on a chair, staring at a fire offstage which is casting the reddish reflections of flames on his face. The Mahatma appears and, placing a comforting hand on Mohan's shoulder, also stares in the same direction.

MAHATMA: Why are you stunned? Death in prison is no different from death outside. Kasturba has only followed your secretary Mahadev Desai into the great beyond.

MOHAN: What am I going to do now?

MAHATMA: Continue as before—

MOHAN: But without her.

MAHATMA: Death is as much a part of life as life is of death.

MOHAN: Her body is taking a long time to burn. The flames of the funeral pyre are gentle with her.

MAHATMA: You could go to your room and rest but...

MOHAN: How can I leave her during her last moments on earth? (*Chuckles*) She would never forgive me if I did.

MAHATMA: (*Also chuckling*) She was always looking for ways to set you straight.

MOHAN: Thank God, we found the saree she loved.

MAHATMA: She loved it because you spun it for her with your own hands.

MOHAN: White cotton with a red border. I called it her birthday saree.

MAHATMA: It is burning with her. That is the way of all matter.

MOHAN: Only the spirit remains.

MAHATMA: Or does it?

MOHAN: The *Gita* says fire does not burn it nor water wet it.

MAHATMA: We will all arrive at that truth one day and know it or not know it.

MOHAN: I shall be so alone.

MAHATMA: You have … me.

MOHAN: (*Chuckles*) It is the prerogative of madmen and mahatmas to talk to themselves.

MAHATMA: That's right, look on the funny side of things.

MOHAN: Guide me. Help me. To know the right action. To do the right thing.

MAHATMA: The means must be in consonance with the end. If the end is to be good, the means must be good. Beware the argument that begins with the phrase "In the national interest". It is usually an attempt to justify bad means leading to an unethical act that goes against humanity.

MOHAN: The fight becomes more difficult with every passing day. Prejudice masquerades as religion.

MAHATMA: Not unexpected. You encouraged it.

MOHAN: Did I?

MAHATMA: You made politics a numbers game. You involved large masses of people in the struggle. Now no one talks to each other except through the crowd.

The lights fade.

SCENE 24

A spot comes on to show Sarojini. She is obviously in mid-speech to a public gathering.

SAROJINI: A new government has been voted to power in Britain. It has promised India freedom! (*Unfurling a flag*) And here is the Indian tricolour!

The sound of a crowd cheering. Sarojini blows kisses to the imaginary crowd. The spot fades. Another comes on.

JINNAH: If the British government is to quit India, then it must divide and quit. Partition the country. Pakistan for the Muslims, Hindustan for the Hindus.

Another spot.

MOHAN: No. India for all Indians.

Another spot.

JAWAHAR: India for all. A secular, socialist republic.
JINNAH: A religious Islamic state—Pakistan! Now, look here, you fellows, let us get this straight. You represent the Hindus and I represent the Muslims.
MOHAN: No, we represent the people of India, whether Hindu, Muslim or whatever. You represent only those Muslims who belong to the Muslim League.

JAWAHAR: A majority of the Muslims of India are not members of the League. Many are members of the Congress. As proof I offer this: in 1937 the Muslim League won only 23% of the Muslim seats in the various legislatures of India. In other words, 77% of India's Muslims were not with the League. Out of 485 reserved Muslim seats, only 108 were won by the Muslim League.

JINNAH: This is all nit-picking. More and more Muslims will join the League by and by.

MOHAN: Let us sit together and talk.

JINNAH: By all means.

JAWAHAR: Unfortunately, the Gandhi-Jinnah talks have failed. The Simla Conference has failed. The Cabinet Mission is here. It consists of three wise men and true, sent by Clement Atlee, the prime minister heading the new Labour government in Britain. Let us at least agree on an interim government for India and get used to the exercise of power.

JINNAH: Very well, if you allot some seats to the Muslim League.

JAWAHAR: Certainly. Out of the twelve seats, we are leaving two to be filled by appointees of the Muslim League.

JINNAH: That's ridiculous! That doesn't give proportional representation to the Muslims of India.

JAWAHAR: But you don't represent all the Muslims of India. We have seen that in the pattern of all the elections since 1937.

JINNAH: Well then, what you will see now is not nimby-pimby Civil Disobedience but Direct Action.

JAWAHAR: Just a minute. Why don't you discuss it all with the new viceroy, Lord Mountbatten.

JINNAH: (*Smiles*) I know how well you get on with…the Mountbattens. Everyone knows. There are rumours.

JAWAHAR: (*Sharply*) What do you mean? Are you implying that—?

JINNAH: Nothing, dear Jawahar. I am implying nothing. I know you well enough to imply nothing. All I am saying, quite clearly, is that everyone knows you've asked Mountbatten to be the first governor-general of free India.

JAWAHAR: (*Relieved*) Ah. Yes. That. The Congress felt it would be an appropriate gesture and help to maintain the continuity of the Indo-British relationship.

JINNAH: Indeed. Indeed. It would help to keep it going. It would help to keep them here. Great fun and all that.

JAWAHAR: I assure you that Dickie is not likely to let any other consideration bias his thinking. His answer is bound to be of great consequence to the subcontinent.

JINNAH: Very well then, let's ask him.

A spot comes on to reveal Mountbatten.

MOUNTBATTEN: Well now, I'm not really concerned with the details. What I *am* concerned with is the stability of India and its Armed Forces. We've already had problems with Subhas Bose who went over to the Germans and Japanese in order to set up a rebel Indian National Army. Now, we've just had a mutiny of the Indian ratings of the Royal Indian Navy. I don't think we can hang on much longer and, frankly, we have no wish to. Decide your destinies. Whether you agree together or not, we quit.

The spot on him fades.

JAWAHAR: Jinnah, I really think we should come to some agreement. What do you say?
JINNAH: (*A slight pause*) We must have Pakistan.
JAWAHAR: Now, look here, old fellow, we really must discuss this sensibly—
JINNAH:: I think it's time for Direct Action Day.

As the lights fade, there are sounds of rioting, carnage, looting, gunfire, explosions, shouts and cries and weeping.

A spot comes on to show Mohan anguished by the sounds, looking one way then the other. A man who is obviously Muslim runs in.

MAN ONE: Bapu! Bapu! There are communal riots in Noakhali. I speak to you on behalf of the Muslims. Both Hindus and Muslims are killing each other. No one is safe. What shall we do? Save us.

MOHAN: Take me to Noakhali. I shall walk the village roads and ask for peace.

Another man, obviously a Hindu, runs in from another direction.

MAN TWO: Mahatma ji! Mahatma ji! I come to you on behalf of the hindus. Help us. In Bihar, there is killing and rape and plunder.
MOHAN: I shall come there, too. After Noakhali. Come, walk with me, first in Noakhali, then in Bihar.
MAN TWO: (*Hesitates*) It is not safe.
MOHAN: (*To Man One*) Will you?
MAN ONE: I am ... afraid.
MOHAN: Then I shall walk alone. You know, the poet Tagore wrote a song in Bengali which I like very much. It says, "If no one will walk with you, walk alone—akla chalo, akla chalo, akla chalo re!"

He starts to walk away. The two men look at each other then turn to Mohan.

MAN ONE: I'll walk with you.
MAN TWO: So will I.
MOHAN: Let's walk the roads and stop the fighting. Let's walk the roads and still the storm.

As they walk away, we hear the sound of many voices joining in to sing Tagore's song. Another spot comes up very slowly on Jinnah as the singing fades away.

JINNAH: There is no alternative to partition. There are two Muslim majority areas in the north west and north east of India. These would constitute Pakistan.

JAWAHAR: We have waited too long for freedom to let it be postponed any more. There seems no alternative to partition. Even Sardar Patel, the so-called strong man of India, says, "A government at odds with itself wouldn't work. It's better to let the Muslim League go its own way. Perhaps there's no alternative to partition."

A spot comes on to show Mohan.

MOHAN: But there is!

They turn towards the sound of his voice, startled.

JINNAH: There is?
JAWAHAR: What do you mean, Bapu?
JINNAH: What alternative can there be?
MOHAN: The unity of the country is at stake. This is not the time for quibbling. After all, it's only about power and who forms the government, isn't it?

They look at each other uncertainly, then each in his own way nods.

JINNAH: Obviously.

JAWAHAR: Yes, of course.

MOHAN: Well then, let Jinnah form the government of India and let him head it.

JINNAH: What?

JAWAHAR: Good heavens!

MOHAN: Why not? If Jinnah and the Muslim League are so scared of being swamped by the majority, then let them form the government and protect the values they hold dear. But don't partition the land. If you do, you set up two armed camps in constant conflict. Don't partition.

JAWAHAR: (*Softly*) Bapu, have you gone mad? And there are other problems too, like the princes and which side they each will join.

MOHAN: Sardar Patel is talking to the princes. He can tackle that. But, as for this, I say let Jinnah form the government.

JAWAHAR: You astound me. Have you mentioned this to Patel?

MOHAN: (*Chuckles*) He thought it was a ridiculous, preposterous idea, impossible to work with. He said, "Beware, dear Gandhiji, you are making yourself redundant."

JAWAHAR: Sometimes one can't but agree with him. We shall vote. Bapu, you will be isolated.

MOHAN: Don't partition. I tell you, there will be a flood of blood.

JINNAH: Partition and be done with it. Jawahar, tell the British we agree. They should divide and quit.

JAWAHAR: Alright, Jinnah, we agree.

MOHAN: (*Deeply pained*) Oh, this is no joy to me. (He turns away)

A spot comes on to reveal Mountbatten.

MOUNTBATTEN: Very well, then, Partition it shall be. Divide your assets. 15th August 1947, independence for India. 16th August 1947, the birth of Pakistan.

JAWAHAR: Freedom at last.

MOHAN: What freedom?

JINNAH: Celebrate.

MOHAN: Celebrate what? Riots have already broken out at the announcement of partition. What I feared is happening. In the next few months more people may be killed here than in the two world wars in Europe. Millions will be uprooted, rendered homeless. Already, whole caravans of refugees are being butchered. Trainloads are being massacred. I am going to Calcutta to try and quell the riots there. This is not the independence I sought.

Mohan leaves.

JINNAH: But the question is, whether it was possible or practicable to act otherwise than what has been done

... A division had to take place. On both sides, in Hindustan and Pakistan, there are sections of people who may not agree with it, who may not like it, but in my judgement there was no other solution and I am sure future history will record its verdict in favour of it. And what is more it will be proved by actual experience as we go on that that was the only solution ... Any idea of a United India could never have worked and in my judgement it would have led us to terrific disaster. May be that view is correct; maybe it is not; that remains to be seen.

JAWAHAR: At the stroke of the midnight hour, while the whole world sleeps, India will awake to life and freedom.

The sound of jubilant crowds, celebrating and shouting "Azadi! Azadi! Freedom! Freedom! Mahatma Gandhi zindabad! Long live Mahatma Gandhi! Long live Pandit Nehru! Long live Mountbatten!" The sounds fade and we hear the sounds of rioting and bloodshed.

SCENE 25

Sarojini with Lord Mountbatten.

MOUNTBATTEN: It's good of you to bring me news of him. We missed him sorely at the festivities. Tell me, how did he celebrate?

SAROJINI: Gandhiji spent Independence Day alone in Calcutta, fasting and praying. He is a deeply troubled man, a shell of himself. He seems shaken by the horror of the prejudice he sees running rampant among the people he has helped become free. Is it freedom, he wonders, if the mind is still slave to religious prejudice and the urge to violence?

MOUNTBATTEN: Isn't it amazing? In Punjab, we have an army of 100,000 and we have riots and bloodshed. In Calcutta, there is a one-man force in the shape of Mahatma Gandhi and we have absolute peace.

Jawahar enters.

JAWAHAR: (*To Sarojini*) Ah, there you are, my dear!

Jawahar greets her with a namaste. She responds in the same way.

MOUNTBATTEN: Well, Mrs. Naidu, if you'll excuse me, I'll leave you in the prime minister's competent hands. There are a few things that even a governor general can't put off.

SAROJINI: (*Laughs*) Yes, of course. And thank you very much for looking after me so kindly.

Mountbatten leaves.

JAWAHAR: Welcome to Delhi, my dear Sarojini, though I can hardly think of it anymore as the Delhi we've all known.

SAROJINI: Oh?

JAWAHAR: It's absolutely ruined, I'm afraid, by some of the most horrible rioting and bloodshed. You must've seen the parks and pavements choked with refugees. We're billeting them on everyone who has any room. Tents are being pitched in gardens. But, unfortunately, some of those who have suffered elsewhere come here and extract their revenge. It's terrible! The place is full of the most wicked characters spewing hatred. What we need is the calming influence of Gandhiji and his multi-denominational prayer-meetings. I've begged him to come here soon and I hope he will.

SAROJINI: He's on his way.

JAWAHAR: Thank heavens. You know, on top of everything else we're having a problem with Pakistan about the division of the assets. They say we haven't given them all we should. But, dash it, we've given them their entire country, haven't we?

SAROJINI: How much more is Jinnah asking for?

JAWAHAR: Fifty-five crores.

SAROJINI: That's five hundred and fifty million rupees.

JAWAHAR: Correct. We can't afford it. We just can't. I've left it to Sardar Patel to answer.

SAROJINI: And what has he told Jinnah?

JAWAHAR: In effect, to suck eggs. He's like that. Blunt.

SAROJINI: Hm. I suppose there's nothing Jinnah can do about it.

JAWAHAR: (*Shrugs*) What can he do? (*Irritated*) Dash it, this just isn't the time to be fiddling with details and accounting books! We're in the middle of a major upheaval. It's all Jinnah's fault, anyway.

The lights fade.

SCENE 26

Mohan seated crosslegged, swaying slightly as though entranced by some inner delight. He is at a prayer-meeting facing the audience. The music of a rhythmic bhajan fades. He opens his eyes.

MOHAN: Nothing would please me more than to die in the cause of communal harmony. I have always been opposed to the partition of the country but now that it has happened with the concurrence of leaders on both sides, it is only right and proper that the division of the assets must be done precisely and correctly. If the treasury owes fifty-five crore rupees to Pakistan, then it must be paid. If necessary, I shall go on a fast to support the claim of Pakistan. I am told that it is not in the national interest to pay the money. But I tell you there is no national interest higher than abiding by the truth. However much it may seem to hurt us, we must stick to the moral principle.

Another bhajan or hymn begins to be played and voices join in the singing. Mohan closes his eyes and sways gently to the music. The lights fade.

SCENE 27

Two men—Godse and Pahwa—enter somewhat nervously and uncertainly.

GODSE: This place will do. Where is it?
PAHWA: What?
GODSE: The round thing. The target.

Pahwa searches in his pockets and brings out a folded sheet of paper. He unfolds it. On it is a slipshod bullseye drawn with crayons.

PAHWA: It's not very tidy.
GODSE: It'll do. (*Looks about to see there's no one watching*) We'll have to be quick. Maybe I'll fire just a couple of rounds.
PAHWA: I tested it. It's accurate.
GODSE: But I've got to be sure. Alright. (*Looking offstage*) That tree is perfect. Go and pin it on the tree at chest level. Down there. Go on.
PAHWA: (*Going offstage*) This one?
GODSE: No, the other. Just a little further. That's right. Now come back here. (*A slight pause*) Oh oh, it's fallen off.
PAHWA: (*Offstage*) Shall I go back and stick it on again?

GODSE: No, forget it. I'll just aim for the tree. Come on, hurry up.

Pahwa returns and stands by as Godse takes out a pistol. He takes careful aim at the offstage target and fires twice.

PAHWA: It fires alright.
GODSE: But it's not accurate. It missed the target.
PAHWA: (*Peering offstage*) But both bullets hit the tree.
GODSE: That's the wrong tree, you fool. I knew it was wrong to rely on you to supply the weapon.
PAHWA: You'll just have to get closer to him, that's all. I'm sure it's not difficult. He refuses to have any security around him. Go up to him and greet him. He's a mahatma, after all. Get his blessings before you shoot him.
GODSE: (*Putting the pistol away*) You're quite a funny fellow. But you're right. He is a mahatma. (*Then with growing anger*) But he's making weaklings of us Hindus. All this non-violence is not good for us. He sides with the muslims. He's destroying this country. He let Partition happen. Why didn't he fast against Partition? But no, he threatens to fast for Pakistan's right to our money. And now Nehru and Patel have immediately delivered fifty-five crores of rupees to Pakistan.
PAHWA: Shoot the swine.

The lights fade.

SCENE 28

The sound of the ramdhun being played and sung. Mohan, accompanied by a small group, enters and begins to cross. The Mahatma enters at a tangent.

MAHATMA: So, Mohan, this is it.

The scene freezes. Mohan breaks away from the group.

MOHAN: This is what?

MAHATMA: We can discuss this later as actors. But for now…be brave.

MOHAN: Courage comes from doing what you believe in.

MAHATMA: Well said. For a frightened little boy scared of the dark, you have scaled the greatest height—yourself. Last week a bomb was thrown at the prayer-meeting. You didn't ask for increased security or police protection.

MOHAN: Why are you reminding me of all this? I want to put it out of my mind.

MAHATMA: Very well. But this will make it stick in everyone's mind.

MOHAN: (*Chuckles*) I'm late for the prayer-meeting.

MAHATMA: You are in time for history.

The Mahatma disappears. The scene unfreezes. One or two persons greet Mohan. Godse enters from the direction in which

Mohan is going. He bends down as though to touch Mohan's feet. Mohan stops and does namaste. Godse brings up his own joined palms as though in namaste. Then lets the pistol come into view. The moment seems to freeze. Then three shots ring out.

MOHAN: Hey Ram!

As he sinks down, a woman helps lower his body to the ground. A couple of policemen run in and disarm the stunned Godse quickly and pin his arms behind him. Nehru and Mountbatten rush in and stand aghast. Godse is led away by the policemen. Suddenly all exclamations and weeping stop. The ramdhun stops. The scene freezes.

The Mahatma appears. He looks down at Mohan cradled by his followers. It is like the pieta.

MAHATMA: I am a shadow. The shadow of an actor. (*The Mahatma reaches down and helps Mohan to rise.*) An actor in a drama beyond time.

As Mohan and the Mahatma leave together, the scene unfreezes. The ramdhun is heard. There is the sound of weeping and wailing. Jawaharlal Nehru moves a few steps forward.

JAWAHAR: The light has gone out of our lives and there is darkness everywhere. The light has gone out, I said, and yet I was wrong. For the light that has shone in this country was no ordinary light. The light that has illumined this country for these many, many years will illumine this country for many more years, and a thousand years later, that light will still be seen in this country and the world will see it and it will give solace to innumerable hearts. For that light represented something more than the immediate present, it represented the living, the eternal truths...

The actors line up, shoulder to shoulder, and take a bow, then part at the centre, turn and gesture upstage as Mohan and the Mahatma join them and, together, they all take a bow.

CURTAIN